Buying and Renovating Houses for Profit

BUYING AND RENOVATING HOUSES FOR PROFIT

K Ludman and R D Buchanan

THE
KOGAN PAGE
Working for Yourself
SERIES

Copyright © K Ludman and R D Buchanan 1984

All rights reserved

First published in Great Britain in 1984
by Kogan Page Limited
120 Pentonville Road
London N1 9JN

British Library Cataloguing in Publication Data

Ludman, K.
  Buying and renovating houses for profit.
  1. House buying—Great Britain   2. House
  selling—Great Britain   3. Dwellings—
  Great Britain—Remodelling
  I. Title   II. Buchanan, R.
  333.33'8   HD1379

  ISBN 0-85038-840-6
  ISBN 0-85038-841-4 Pbk

Printed in Great Britain by the Anchor Press
and bound by William Brendon & Son Ltd, both
of Tiptree, Essex

Contents

Introduction

It may seem strange that we should be suggesting at this time of great unemployment that there is a relatively secure, inflation-proof way of earning a living; amid prophecies of doom from the economists, many people are repeatedly being told that they will be unlikely to have a job again in their whole lifetime, let alone earn a decent wage. Even the envisaged upturn in the country's fortunes is no guarantee of more jobs being created; in fact, microchips and computerisation have permanently removed the need for the vast (and now expensive) work-forces which have been commonplace since the industrial revolution.

But we are suggesting just this. Restoring old houses keeps a large section of the building trade in lucrative employment. As a building grows older the more maintenance it needs and, although the evil day can be put off by the owner, when the time for repairs inevitably comes around, the bill is even bigger than it would have been for repairs carried out regularly.

Why, then, is this form of employment so much more secure than others? Because people must have houses to live in, and they demand a certain minimum level of comfort; this level may vary between different income groups but it remains constant through wide changes in the economic conditions of the country. For example, a high court judge and an assembly line worker, however different much of their daily lives may be, will both expect at the end of a day's work to go home to a comfortable, weatherproof home with central heating and pleasant decor. Even the tenants in council properties expect this, and usually get it. People have the need to feel secure and comfortable 'within their own four walls', so there is always a steady flow of people moving from rented accommodation to a place of their own.

The building trade is therefore a good source of income in relation to renovating older houses but it has its drawbacks. A competent one- or two-man building concern may earn a very good wage doing this kind of work but, owing to the nature of the operation, it is susceptible to loss of earnings due to bad weather and last minute changes of schedule by clients, on which one often has no redress. The small builder is more vulnerable to these problems than a craftsman employed by a large firm which can move labour to another project in the event of a delay of this kind, and so is his pay packet.

The solution to this problem is to buy, restore and sell properties. If you are able to do building work yourself (or even if not) this occupation will give you an income, during the course of each project, lasting several months. The problems encountered by the small builder will be avoided because *you* will be scheduling your work, not someone else, and delays on one job need not put a stop to progress; simply move on to another aspect of the renovation.

If an old property in need of repairs is purchased at a price appropriately below the market value of one in sound condition, one is then in a position to guarantee oneself work, and payment, over the period of time it takes to make it fit for sale at a profit. In other words, you can be a property developer!

Bricks and mortar have always been reckoned the most consistently reliable means of investment: better than savings, and more tangible and predictable than stocks and shares; once you have bought a property, it is yours. You can see it as proof of your investment, and do not merely have to rely on certificates or pieces of paper alone, as with so many others. A property investment has the advantage that the building which you have purchased will almost certainly start to increase in value from the moment you acquire it. This process will continue during your ownership irrespective of the renovation which you will be carrying out.

While it is unlikely that we shall see the kind of property booms where prices nearly double in three to four years, as in the last several decades, it is very seldom that property prices fall.

These, then, are two good reasons for the financial viability of the exercise.

Your suitability for the job

You will want to know, armed with the above information, how it can be of use to *you*.

You may be unemployed and you may know nothing about the building trade. How could it be possible for you to tackle a job like this?

Or you may already have a job which provides a steady income. Why would you want to branch out on your own and be self-employed? It's fair enough for someone who is already a bricklayer or carpenter, who simply wants to put their career in a stronger position, but a complete change of job may seem a bit drastic.

A moment's thought may help. *Anyone* who has a reasonable flair as a handyman could make a go of it, if he is prepared to put some effort into learning the various aspects of the job which we set out in later chapters. If you're not skilled in that area you could still supervise the work at any one of several levels of involvement, depending on what you really want out of it. This can range from being at the heart of the project in every way and at every stage, to merely putting up the capital and doing it as a spare-time activity.

Being out of work need not necessarily be an obstacle to becoming a property developer. Money is available much more easily than most people realise, if you organise the scheme well enough on paper to convince a potential backer — for example your bank manager or an enthused relative with spare cash to invest — that you mean business.

And if you already have a job, maybe your boss has just junked a dozen more of your brilliant ideas and you're thinking it's about time that all your creative effort should be used to greater effect.

11

If you're already self-employed, maybe you're stuck in the same predictable office routine day after day with no opportunity to meet new people; or you may be out on the road all day meeting too many new people and never spending enough time in one place.

Property renovation could be the thing for you in this case. As the kingpin in the project, you will have a good opportunity to set it up in the way *you* prefer to work, with as few or as many people involved as you wish (within reason). This activity gives plenty of free rein for one's ideas, a chance to meet a variety of people including vendors and purchasers of the properties you are involved with, considerable freedom in your daily movements (within the framework of work programmes), and a healthy balance of the indoor and outdoor life, physical exercise and mental effort. Instant access to the fresh air is quite a plus in any job.

Property renovation is one of the relatively few occupations which require no qualifications such as degrees, diplomas, City and Guilds etc. In fact, many of the people doing it are the kind who, while not stupid, do not really fit into this system. There is a lot of room for you if you like to be truly independent.

Such are the good points in favour of the work, but as with anything, there is the less attractive side.

If one is employing people one soon learns that there are some very tough, unhelpful and unreliable characters in the building trade.They can always be replaced, but it takes fairly strong character and determination to deal with the rogues and, in the course of your efforts to lift your house bodily out of the doldrums of neglect into the bliss of rebirth, you will have to do a lot of very hard, sometimes dirty work, much of it under pressure.

The key to success is the will to succeed, first and foremost. But this must be backed up by the right groundwork. The project for each property must be carefully prepared at the outset: research into areas for possible purchases must be thorough, and you must maintain the standard set for yourself at this stage right through until the property is resold, when you can take a (quick) breath. It means being prepared to keep working hard when it might seem very easy to stop.

The rewards, however, are immense. Apart from the steady, fulfilling employment during the course of the work, the potential for additional profits from the sale of the property plus the satisfaction of selling a home to people who are pleased to buy it from you add up to a pleasant feeling of achievement from a job well done.

Chapter 1
Starting

Having read the introduction you now have some idea of your suitability and aptitude for the business of property renovation.

The business comes under three broad headings of property purchase; renovation and conversion; selling/marketing.

Assets

One of the first things you need to do is to find out what you are worth. You must look carefully at your assets as these will play an important part in setting yourself up in business. Don't dismiss yourself as having 'nothing of value'. It is always surprising to find out what you are worth once you sit down and make a list of everything you own.

Assets can be cash; savings—which include building society accounts, premium bonds, local authority and other bonds; insurance policies; valuable articles such as antiques and jewellery, etc. Of course, you don't necessarily have to sell valuable items in order to raise money on them. If you own your own house then that is a valuable asset and will enable you to raise money in the form of a second mortgage. Friends and relatives with capital can also be an asset. (See Chapter 2.)

You may feel by now that you will have to give up everything you own in order to set yourself up in business. This is not the case. You merely need to know what you are worth so that you can decide how much of your own capital you wish to put into your business, and so that you can present a financial picture of yourself to others who may agree to invest in you.

Renovation or conversion?

Before you think about actually raising capital you will need to aquaint yourself with the housing market generally and areas in particular. Choosing the right property to buy is one of the most important parts of the project.

First decide whether you wish to convert into separate flats, or perhaps just to renovate and update a property as a single unit. Both schemes have their merits. Converting a property into flats will inevitably mean more work, more expense and more time. The advantage is that the rewards are usually greater. Also, when converting into flats you will need to make an application to the local authority for 'change of use'. This will involve a planning application supported by detailed drawings, for which you will need an architect. You will not be allowed to start any major work on the property until you have planning permission, which normally takes a few weeks, although in the meantime there are certain things you can be getting on with, such as external painting, pointing of brickwork, garden landscaping, etc.

Renovating a property as one unit (ie, restoring a house to its original condition), however, does not require a change of use application, and you would therefore be able to start work on it immediately. Plans do have to be submitted, however, if you intend adding bathrooms or altering drainage.

The advantages of being able to start work straight away are obvious. You will not be accruing interest unnecessarily on any loans you may have, and your initial enthusiasm can be used to the full.

You will have to decide for yourself which scheme to choose, but bear in mind that you will almost certainly make more profit from conversion into flats.

With this information in mind you can now pick an area.

Areas

There is a lot to be said for choosing an area that you already know, or better still, where you already live.

The reason is that you will already be aware—maybe even without realising it—of the market generally. You will know roughly what houses are worth, and checking on a few that are advertised in estate agents' windows will help to confirm your assessment. You will also have some idea of the type of accommodation that is popular, whether flats, bedsits or large family houses. We ourselves found it much easier to operate in our own area because we had knowledge of local estate agents, we knew the location of builders' merchants and materials suppliers' which cut out a lot of unnecessary travelling—and supervision of the site was made much easier—very worthwhile especially if you employ contractors and are not always on the site yourself.

Nevertheless, if you decide to select an area you don't know, you must first research it very thoroughly.

You may be tempted, for example, to buy a property in a remote country area unknown to you. Some country properties, especially cottages, look ideal for someone starting a renovation business. They are also normally cheaper than properties in towns and cities. It is still possible to buy a really run-down but salvageable property for around £2000, but there has to be a reason why it is so cheap. It could be next to a glue factory or a pig farm, or there could be land subsidence.

Whichever property you choose to buy, you must be sure that you will have a market for it once you have spent thousands of pounds on modernisation. Also, you must gear the renovation to the type of market it will attract. In the case of country cottages, for example, too much money spent on too much renovation will price you out of the 'weekend cottage' market, which in some areas may be the only outlet for your property. So thorough research is important.

As a guide, we have listed the types of property which are worth considering, and those which you ought to avoid.

Best buys

In towns and cities

1. Large, older properties, with garden if possible, which are in a generally run-down condition but are basically sound. These properties readily convert into flats comprising one, two or three bedrooms, and as many flats as possible should have use of the garden. Flats like these are always in demand, and a high proportion go to first-time buyers—newly married couples, etc: a very strong market.

To encourage first-time buyers, the flats need to be nicely converted with good separate access to each one, and have a sound basic standard of workmanship and finish. Avoid being too lavish. Goldfish ponds and sunken baths look very attractive, but the extra money you spend on installing them could put your otherwise very saleable flats out of reach of first-time buyers, and if you can't sell quickly you will be losing money.

2. Small, older houses, again preferably with garden. Gardens are always a good selling point, as you will find when you come to market your finished renovation.

The smaller houses are usually two- or three-storey properties with two main rooms per floor and perhaps an extension at the back. As long as the house is basically sound (this means that no major underpinning or rebuilding of main walls will be necessary) the more neglected it is the better (and cheaper) it is for you to buy.

Small houses are more suitable for renovation and modernisation to make one living unit—ie, not flats—although the actual size and number of rooms is the key factor when deciding what you should do.

In order to make a small house attractive to buyers as a single dwelling, it is necessary to have at least two bedrooms of reasonable size and, if you can manage it, a third bedroom even if you can only just squeeze a single bed into it. You should be able to provide a bathroom (not just a shower room) as near as possible to the bedrooms, and a light, attractive kitchen.

With older period properties, interesting features such as fireplaces and ceiling cornices should be retained.

This type of house will generally be suitable for couples moving from smaller accommodation (flats), families, and single people moving upmarket (from flats, etc). So you should try to keep your potential buyer in mind when looking at properties, as this will be of benefit to you when you come to do the actual renovation work.

Just a word about large houses modernised to make one dwelling: there is a market for this type of property, of course, but people buying a large renovated house have a lot of money to spend and are going to be conscious of area and position and will want a very high standard of finish and decor. The capital outlay and the amount of work involved is likely to be too much for a first-time project—so we will forget them for the time being.

When looking at properties in towns and cities, try and imagine what it would be like to live there yourself. Keep in mind that people have to travel to work, buy food etc. A lot of people choose to come and live in an area because they can get to work easily. So when selecting properties to buy, look carefully at how close they are to bus and rail stations, shops, schools, parks etc, and try to avoid properties on busy main roads, which are often noisy and dirty. Most people would rather live in a quiet side street near amenities rather than on top of them.

Location is very important.

Country properties

As already mentioned, small country cottages are usually cheaper to buy than town properties. Suitable properties are:

1. Secluded or remote cottages in a poor state of repair. Some cottages are so small that you will be able to carry out quite major work at a fraction of the cost of a similar project in town or city. But you must be careful not to spend too much in relation to what the property is worth, otherwise your mark-up (the

difference between what you spend and what you actually receive after sale) is likely to be so minimal that the whole exercise will have been futile.

Country cottages will attract people looking for a second home or possibly a retirement home. In this situation people can afford to spend a long time looking for their perfect home as there is not the same pressure on them to move—in contrast with flats in towns and cities, for example, where buyers normally need to buy and move quickly, possibly because they have an existing property to sell, or they cannot afford the time off work anyway. So if you are tempted to renovate a country cottage, bear in mind that it could take a long time to sell and that your money will be tied up in it until it is sold.

2. Houses in small towns and villages. These can be worth considering but again there is unlikely to be the pressure on people to buy. The market is not so clearly defined. The only certain way of assuring a sale is to have a buyer lined up before you start. The buyer can then specify his renovation requirements in advance. However, setting up a deal in this way means that, in order to protect you, your buyer will have to sign a contract agreeing to buy the property after renovation. If all this can be arranged it would be a very satisfactory deal for you as you will know all the costs involved, including the sale price.

Summary of best buys

1. Houses in quiet roads in towns and cities, and near amenities. Terraced or semi-detached and suitable for conversion into flats. Proximity to commercial area (eg, central London) along with good travel facilities.

2. Any small house near a business or commercial area and amenities. Terraced or semi-detached, and suitable for renovation as a single dwelling or conversion to small flats or bed-sit accommodation. Again, good travel facilities.

3. Houses in areas which are starting to become fashionable—a lot of people will want to move into these areas.

4. Country cottages within a few hours' drive of a city centre. They should be quiet and secluded but have easy access to major roads.

Other factors contribute to the suitability of a property. They are:

A garage—good selling point

On-street parking (no meters)

South-facing garden—gets a lot of sun

Cul-de-sac—no through traffic makes these streets pleasant to live in.

Summary of bad buys

1. Houses in depressed areas. Prices will drop rather than improve. People are moving away because the area is no longer fashionable. You might be able to buy cheaply but you would never be able to sell at the price you required.

2. Listed buildings. You would have to renovate them the way somebody else wanted—not the way you wanted. This is time-consuming and profit-losing. Buildings are listed because they have some architectural or historical merit and, if you want to alter them in any way, approval has to be sought from the listed buildings authority.

The same restrictions apply to a lesser degree in conservation areas. Conservation areas are declared by the local council when it wishes to retain the character and amenities of an area and control any development within it. Converting a property in a conservation area will usually take longer and cost more, but it has to be said that many people like the benefits of living in such an area, so there would not necessarily be a problem in selling your property— only in converting it. Ask your local authority what would be required before you buy.

3. Any property which is in an area that is going to be redeveloped on a large scale, or has major road improvements planned for it. Check with planning authorities.

Additional points to watch for:

Avoid main roads—especially very busy ones

Don't consider houses near factories/workshops etc

Don't consider houses a long way from shops and/or public transport

Avoid houses with major structural faults such as collapsed drains and foundations

Avoid houses adjacent to overhead railways.

Your legal position

In setting up your own business you will have to consider your tax position.

If you intend to work full time at property renovation, and work alone, then you will become self-employed (unless you are already).

Should you form a partnership with others you will probably consider forming a company, as this puts you and the others on a sound legal footing. You can either buy an existing company which has ceased trading, or set up a new one from scratch. Buying an existing company is cheaper, but you may have to change the memorandum and articles of association, which can cost money. Once the company is formed you will have to decide whether to be a company employee and pay yourself a wage, deducting tax under PAYE, or whether to choose self-employed status. Either way you can be a company director. Your accountant will advise which is best for you.

It is not a good idea to buy a going concern—ie, a company already trading in property renovation.

Whether you decide to work alone or with others, the following points are worth remembering:

1. If you form a partnership with others they will want to be involved in decision-making. This can waste time and may mean that you disagree on working methods etc. So if you must form a partnership—keep the numbers as small as possible.

2. A company will cost money and time to set up and run. Annual returns have to be made to Companies

House. Returns for corporation tax have to be made and, as a property company, you will find it difficult to register for VAT. Certain home improvements such as central heating, previously zero rated, now attract VAT at the standard rate. You will also have to hold regular company meetings and produce minutes for which you will need a company secretary.

3. Local authority grants may be harder to obtain as a property company.

4. A definite advantage of a limited company is that it has limited liability. This means that in any legal action taken against your company, the claim is limited to the face value of the company shares, and does not involve you personally. Solicitors can advise on company law, more about which in Chapter 12.

5. As a sole trader you will run the whole business yourself, the profit will be greater, and the day-to-day running of the business will be easier.

Any property you buy will have to be insured against damage, theft of materials and tools, and damage to persons and other property. Property insurance and public liability insurance are dealt with in Chapter 12, and are not as formidable as they sound.

At some stage you will need to appoint solicitors, who can do as much or as little as you want them to. It is likely that they will handle conveyancing (buyer's contracts, local authority searches etc) of your properties. They can also arrange the formation of your company, act as company secretary, and offer advice on any legal problems which crop up. (There are always a few.) If you already know a solicitor, all well and good. If not, then get some idea of charges and suitability and shop around before finally deciding.

The local authorities have laws with which you must comply. These are explained in Chapter 12.

You will also have to comply with the requirements of the District Surveyor. He is responsible for making sure that you carry out certain building work to the required standard, and his word is law—so don't upset him.

Presenting yourself

Whether you trade as a company or as an individual you are going to make contact with a lot of people and organisations. You will have to present yourself to banks, solicitors, council departments, materials suppliers and so on. To do this efficiently, business cards and printed letterheads are necessary. You will also need to write letters to many people, offices and official bodies, and for this purpose a neatly laid out letter on headed paper will present a professional image.

You will have to set up a company bank account, from which all transactions relating solely to the business should be handled. Most builders' merchants and materials suppliers will not take a company cheque unless you can produce company headed paper. In order to establish yourself with suppliers, you will need to become known, and the best way to do this is to present your card and headed paper when you buy materials. This way they will know that you are a bona fide trader with a registered company address, and will readily do business with you.

Chapter 2
Raising Capital

Having convinced yourself that the property business is right for you, the next thing you have to do is
raise the money to start. If you have all the necessary
capital to cover the outgoings on the whole project,
this will maximise your profit; there need be no
backers waiting for a share of the profits to diminish
your own, and no bankers charging a steady interest
rake-off on borrowed moneys.

Your own funds

It is always best to use your own funds, in whatever
form, if you have them, rather than someone else's,
which will always cost you.

Other sources

If you do not have all the money you will need, or even
if you have none at all, there are several other sources.
These fall into three categories:

1. Backers and partners
2. Loans
3. Grants.

Backers and partners

Family. There may be members of your family suffi-
ciently keen on the new project to help with some of
their savings—you may be surprised to find that a
great aunt has been wondering how to reinvest her
premium bonds, and only bothers to tell you when she
hears of your proposed enterprise.

Friends. You may find that a friend is prepared to put
up some of the front money to get you started once
you show that you have thought the whole thing

through well enough beforehand; try it out, even on the ones who you think will not show any interest—enthusiasm is infectious even to the cynics, and after you've let them shoot you down in flames a few times, they will be impressed by your persistence if you press on with your plans despite what *they* may consider to be impossible odds. In fact they may well end up putting *their* money where *your* mouth is!

Contacts. If you put the word about among your friends and acquaintances you may well get to hear of someone who is looking for a project to invest money in. It is surprising just how much investment capital is available, but you won't get to hear about it by day-dreaming of yourself as a property magnate and complaining, as so many do, that your talents are not appreciated. *Show* these talents by your efforts to interest people in the venture. Remember that at this stage of the game you will be learning your most difficult lesson—how to present a case involving quantities of money which most people only dream about—but your nervousness about it will be reduced by the relaxed way in which people who are used to putting up considerable sums as backing discuss your problems with you. Pick up on their air of assurance and get to grips with their ways of looking at your 'baby', and you will begin to feel more at ease with what, not long before, may well have seemed even to you a hare-brained scheme.

You will almost certainly turn up some positive results in this area. You must come to an agreement with your backer as to how much return you will give him or her on the investment. One way to arrive at this figure is to arrange to make the backer's share of the profits proportional to his initial stake in the venture; this need not mean that if he puts up, say, 30 per cent of your total capital that he is entitled to collect 30 per cent of the profits. He has a right to expect a greater return on his money than he would get from the safest forms of investment, ie building society or bank deposit accounts (at around 12 per cent gross per year), for he is undeniably taking a greater risk with your venture, but he should also take into account the fact that, in the early projects, you must find your feet financially. It could be that if you commit yourself to giving him a fixed sum at share-out time, before the project starts, the payment of this money on resale of the house leaves you out of pocket.

To summarise: agree on giving backers a share of the profits proportional to their original stake (but trimmed a little to take into account your greater involvement; eg, if you have three backers contributing say 50, 25 and 12 per cent respectively, offer them 40, 20 and 9.6 per cent. This enables you to collect the difference at the share-out, 17.4 per cent of the profits, as a reward for your efforts).

Arrange, if possible, for the profit each backer will receive to be more than he would get with a building society or bank, so if your scheme ties his money up for three months you should offer him more than 3 per cent on his investment. But make sure in your calculations that this is feasible—more about this later.

You should decide at this stage whether to formalise any of these arrangements. Experience tends to show that it is always safer for all concerned to draw up a legal document, form a legally binding partnership or a limited company which commits everyone to the enterprise not only in spirit but also in responsibility. This applies just as much to a joint venture with a close relative as with a more formal, professional body such as a bank.

Sleeping partners. Although raising all your cash from sleeping partners, ie backers who merely contribute their share to the project at the outset and wait for their profit at the end of the job, may seem the best approach, in practice it is difficult for these people to stand aside and resist the temptation to pitch in their own suggestions on how the work should be carried out. This is natural enough, since they probably feel that their money will be that much better looked after if they 'help you' to utilise it well. Hence, the more sleeping partners you have, the greater the risk of the project becoming a tug of war. These problems will be compounded if you also have a poorly defined business relationship because you started out being such close friends.

Working partners. In practice, it may be better to take on at least one working partner. He or she, in addition to contributing a stake, can help with the work and the running of the job.

Difficulties which sometimes arise in joint decision-making in a 50-50 set-up of this kind can be more than offset by the sharing, and hence lightening, of the burden of keeping the job moving. It is really up to you to decide exactly how to tackle this problem of partners and backers, depending on your particular situation and preferences, but the issues mentioned above will help you to consider the most important aspects.

Loans

The most readily available loans for the renovator are from banks and building societies. These organisations are both useful sources of funds but, of course, the money which you borrow from them will be subject to interest charges from day one. Whereas a backer will charge you nothing for the use of his money *during* the project itself, a bank will almost certainly be charging interest daily on borrowed finance and deducting it from your account every three months. This means that any delays during the course of the operation will add to your costs accordingly. However, it is easy to raise money by this means, and the very act of setting about doing it is a healthy astringent to the euphoria which sets in as the project draws nearer to becoming a reality.

Banks. Most bank managers will be very ready to listen to your proposals, but will not contribute all of the funds. They will want to see financial projections (discussed in Chapter 6), and they will expect you to be putting up some front money. One way of doing this, if you have no available capital, is to get together with several partners, each of you contributing an equal stake to a kitty. This kitty can be used as 'share capital'. Form a limited company with your colleagues. Your combined funds in the company represent a measure of commitment and show your ability to get the thing together, and when shown this evidence, your bank manager will be prepared to match this money with two or maybe three times as much.

If you or your partners do not have enough money to make the initial kitty large enough for you to raise all the finance you need by this method, each of you should apply for individual personal loans, or unsecured loans, which are reasonably easy to obtain if you are a householder: you may have to sign a few forms, but you need not commit yourself to signing away the roof over your head or anything drastic. It is still best to go through the banks rather than other means of obtaining credit, as these (ie credit card organisations, etc) charge exorbitant rates of interest.

Thus the money *can* be raised through the bank, though it may be diplomatic to choose as your company bank a different one from that which has provided the unsecured loan(s); if one of your number has no need to borrow his stake, put the company account with his branch.

Your bank manager may prefer you to take out a secured loan or he may offer you an overdraft. If you are already self-employed you may have an existing arrangement with the bank which permits you to overdraw, that is, go into debit on your account up to a pre-arranged limit. It may be possible to extend the limit of this overdraft for the renovation scheme, though do remember that an overdraft facility can be withdrawn without notice. However, it is not a common practice.

With a secured loan you stand a good chance of being able to raise a greater sum of money, but the bank will have a tighter hold over you; the manager will probably want to take a second charge on property which you already own. This means that, should he have any difficulty collecting repayments from you, he *could* recoup the money by claiming a share of your home and demanding it be sold so that he is repaid. This is really only a formality, and the chances of any such uncomfortable proceedings are very remote.

In the case of secured and unsecured loans, and one form of overdraft, repayment is made on a regular (usually monthly) basis, the repayments consisting of principle and interest. The period of repayment is pre-arranged, as is the amount of each instalment. If you run into difficulties, or want the borrowing carried over a longer period, the banks are ready to listen and quite flexible in their approach.

Where you are working on an overdraft allowance the permissible borrowing limit remains the same for the duration but, more important, you will only be charged interest on the amount you are in debit at any given time: unlike loans, the money need not be drawn until the moment you need to use it, so if there are delays you will not be parting with regular repayments which may be hard to find. Also, if you have sources of income other than the renovation, paying these moneys into your overdrawn account will reduce the drain of interest. You do not *have* to make regular repayments anyway with this arrangement, as long as you keep below your limit, although in practice it's best to try to do so.

If all of your finance for the project is borrowed— the funds provided by the bank to your *company* account will almost certainly be on an overdraft allowance basis—it goes without saying that speed will be of the essence in completing the project to keep outgoings on interest payments to the lowest possible level.

Building societies. Of the other possible means of borrowing, a remortgage or second mortgage is the best. If you own a property you can raise capital by mortgaging it for the necessary sum with a building society.

Even if your property is already mortgaged, it may be of sufficient value to enable you to increase the mortgage: the property will probably have increased in value since you purchased it, so that even if you obtained the highest mortgage possible then, its present market value will permit more borrowing by this method.

There are many other methods of raising your capital but for various reasons they are less practical, for example, borrowing from finance houses. The only real alternative which may be available to you is a grant.

Home Improvement Grants

It has been government policy since April 1982 to encourage the awarding of full grants for major repairs to properties in use as domestic accommodation. Grants for basic amenities have also been encouraged. If you feel that in your circumstances it's worthwhile applying for one, here is some basic information to help you through the jungle!

There are several types of local authority home improvement grants. The two most important categories are:

1. Mandatory Grants
2. Discretionary Grants

You are automatically entitled to a Mandatory Grant, which is described as being a grant for 'basic improvements and associated repairs', if your property meets certain universal basic requirements. Discretionary Grants are only given after your particular case has been considered on its own merits. At the time of writing the waiting list for Discretionary Grants is likely to be about 12 months (before the awarding of the grant, not payment of the money!) as a result of changes in government policy since April 1982.

Priority is given to the Mandatory Grants, which can help pay the costs of installing a fixed bath or shower, wash-hand basin, sink, inside toilet and hot and cold water supplies where these facilities do not already exist.

The amount of money you will qualify for is based on a set of tables which are published by the DOE in Housing Booklet No 14. This is very lucid and strongly recommended reading. Each item of work is allocated a sum of money in the tables. This represents the 'eligible expense limit', ie maximum expen-

31

diture that the DOE thinks is reasonable on the work. The amount of money awarded in the grant is then a *percentage* of this figure (90 per cent from April 1982 to April 1984, 75 per cent from April 1984 on—and these are the maximum). Any expenditure over and above this figure will have to be financed by you.

There has been a recent backlash to the government's 'all systems go' attitude—the money had to run out sooner or later, and many councils have a backlog of applications to clear. This situation is exacerbated by the reduction of the maximum grant figure to 75 per cent.

In the present more thrifty atmosphere the large sums of money which have up to now been made available for major structural repairs, especially re-roofing (usually 90 per cent) will totally disappear, as this particular area is covered by the Repairs Grants which are classed as Discretionary. The table will clarify the whole area of Home Improvement Grants.

Conditions attached to grants

Local authority grants for home improvement can be a source of considerable finance but there are two major drawbacks.

First, work must not be started before the grant is awarded, which can mean a wait of two or three months, sometimes longer. Funds from this quarter cannot be relied upon when planning the project, for local authorities often work in mysteriously inconsistent ways. So dicey is the grants system that an acquaintance of ours who has been renovating houses for 15 years has never bothered with them in all that time: remember—if work is held up while you are waiting for final confirmation of the grant, valuable time and money may disappear down the drain with nothing accomplished.

Second, even if you have been able to arrange a grant in record time, maybe before purchasing the property, or if you have been fortunate enough to purchase a property for which a grant (and probably planning permission) has already been obtained by the vendor, the grant money will have to be paid back to the authority if it decides that your renovations are

Category	Type	Eligible expense limit		Maximum amount contributable by local authority
		Greater London	Elsewhere	
Mandatory Local authority *must* award this kind	*Intermediate Grant* Washing and toilet facilities; hot and cold water	£3,005	£2,275	75 per cent from April 1984
Discretionary At local authority's discretion	*Improvement Grant* Major improvements and providing homes by conversion Priority cases Non-priority cases	£13,800 £9,000	£10,200 £6,600	
	Repairs Grant Major structural repairs: roof, walls, floors, foundations	£6,600	£4,800	
	Special Grant	Not applicable for the renovator and converter. Applies only to properties with tenants.		

Local authority home improvement grants

purely a means to the end of reselling the premises as a profit-making venture. At best it is then merely an interest-free loan (but at a price even so—count the hours you end up spending on it, and remember that time is money in this kind of exercise).

There is only one circumstance in which you may keep the grant. If the property is the only one you own, and you are working as a private self-employed individual (or doing the work in your spare time while having another, full-time, job) rather than operating as a limited company, you are less likely to be regarded as undeserving. If you can persuade the authority that you are not specifically renovating for profit—you may want to renovate one house only in the foreseeable future, and sell it after living in it for 10 years or so—there is every chance the authority will not reclaim the grant.

Some councils require you to sign a declaration when applying for a grant; this commits you to paying back the money if you move house within a period of five years (the same period applies throughout the country), although, yet again, interpretation of these rules seems to vary; we know of two contradictory cases which prove the point.

In the first, someone residing in a flat on which she had a mortgage was reluctantly obliged to drop her application for a roof repairs grant (running at up to 90 per cent at that time—1983) because she could not be sure that she would not be moving within the statutory period.

In the second, on the other hand, someone who had sold his own house and bought one to renovate specifically for profit was given a very substantial grant. He subsequently sold the house at a not dissimilar profit, and no claim was made on the grant by the council!

There does seem to be some evidence to show that the local authority, and the taxman, are prepared to go along with this arrangement if it only happens once. Once it becomes a routine though, if house after house is bought and sold with grants used to fund the restoration, council and taxman alike will be at your door for money. You will be regarded as part of 'the private sector', and as such a profit-making concern, undeserving of the ratepayers' assistance. This is really fair enough and observes the general spirit in which local authority aid and the tax laws were drawn up.

To summarise the above, the only means by which you may utilise grants on a regular basis are:

1. If you live on the premises and/or the property is the only one you own.
2. If you do not sell it until the five-year period has elapsed.

This arrangement may be useful to you, although it is unlikely to provide sufficient income if purchase and renovation provide your sole means of employment. Nevertheless, if you are a writer, artist, actor or musician, for instance, or are for other reasons prepared to put up with a subsistence wage for the opportunity it gives you to allocate some of your time to another activity, the freedom to juggle your timetable around may justify the relatively modest returns to be had. But remember that such a drawn-out project is not a good candidate for financing with loans, as the interest charges over such a long period are prohibitive.

It may be possible, even if you are conducting your business as a limited company, to qualify for a grant on *one* of your properties, but one only. If you should get to the stage where you are renovating several properties at once, there is nothing to stop you treating one of these as your own home, applying for grants for it, restoring it and hanging on to it before selling at a profit after five years. In practice you will probably have to live in it anyway, as unoccupied it will be prone to vandalism and will not be paying its way, apart from the ethical objection that habitable dwellings should not be left unoccupied when housing is in such demand. Your grant-aided property will probably have to be run with a separate bank account from the company account to simplify accounting procedures. This is discussed in Chapter 13 under *Using profits*.

Other grants

There are other more remote possibilities under the loose description of grants:

Government aid for small businesses. Complicated.

Department of the Environment (DOE) grants for refurbishing buildings of special historic value. These properties often have striking architectural features—pilasters, colonnades, porticoes etc, and some are centuries old. Applications for Historic Buildings grants present even more of an uphill battle than for Home Improvement grants. The DOE tells us that general policy is to discourage such applications since it is felt that the condition of these properties is reflected in a low purchase price, which is in itself a sufficient perk! Clearly, funds are limited and go only to the really desperate cases.

The government Youth Employment Scheme. You may be tempted to kill two birds with one stone here, availing yourself of a couple of young labourers at the government's expense while helping to reduce the numbers of the nation's unemployed in your own small way. Don't. You will have more than enough on your plate without taking on someone who is new to the world of work and another pile of paperwork to be dealt with.

Chapter 3
Which Property to Buy?

How do you decide which place to buy? There are
several points of which you must make yourself
aware.

The local property market

What is the state of the property market in the area
where you want to renovate? Are prices on the
increase as a result of great demand, or is the locality
already flooded with homes for sale, depressing
prices as a result?

Tour the local estate agents' offices

This will enable you to look at details of properties on
the market—photographs, written descriptions of
layouts, numbers of rooms and dimensions will help
to familiarise you with what's available. You will
soon see that only a small percentage of the
properties for sale will fit all the parameters which
you must apply, and not least of these is the overall
budget for the project. You must base everything else
in the project on the budget, from how much you are
prepared to pay for the house through the total
estimated cost of the work, to other expenses such as
solicitor's, surveyor's and architect's fees, and loan
interest.

Another vital aspect to check out at this stage is the
possible need to apply for permission for a 'change of
use' for the premises, and for planning permission.

Have you found a suitable property?

Does the house you have in mind for the project (there
will probably be one or two which started you

thinking of renovating in the first place) lend itself to improvements and/or alterations without an exorbitant outlay of time and money? Is the end product capable of yielding an adequate profit after all overheads are taken into account (possibly including the interest on loans from banks which will continue to be charged, even when work is completed on the property) until such time as the investment is recouped by resale?

Factors in your choice

Budget
In order to minimise the risk involved (for with any business venture there is always a risk) it is best to keep to as low a budget as possible with the first project. Save the more ambitious possibilities— digging out a basement to put in an extra flat if you are converting, or adding a roof extension to provide another—until you have found your feet on the basics.

The total amount of money needed to finance the operation will depend, first, on the cheapest typical price for a run-down property of the type which lends itself most readily to your purposes. This in turn will depend upon the area in which you choose to buy (see Chapter 1). Additionally, the cost of works must be taken into account, and the time which will be needed to complete them and sell, for this will dictate exactly the outgoings which you must allow for interest payments on loans.

Once your research tour of estate agents' offices has yielded an approximate rock-bottom purchase price for the type of premises you want to buy, you will have the basis for the drawing up of an overall budget.

You must work out a costing comprising all the main items of expenditure on the kind of project you propose to tackle at this stage. These are:

The purchase money
The cost of the works

Fees to solicitors, estate agents, surveyors and architects.
Interest on loans.

More about these shortly, but where do you start with all these calculations? It may seem as if we're suggesting that you have to pull these figures out of thin air.

The method is fairly straightforward: once you have familiarised youself with the types of property available in your proposed area of purchase, and before you get involved in making offers or having surveys carried out, or any other of the preparations for a specific purchase, select *one* house which is as typical as possible of the kind you want for the first project—a good example would be a smallish Victorian property with three floors which might convert into three flats (one storey each) or one flat and one maisonette (two storeys). By deciding on a particular property you will be able to use it to make up a general blueprint which could be applied to any one of a number of houses which you may have your eye on. This is much more practical than wasting time estimating exact costs on one specific house which might be sold to someone else before you could buy it yourself.

You must, in any event, have a budget and plan of campaign drawn up *before* buying the property, otherwise you run the risk of being lumbered with a white elephant; the final selling price of the finished product of your work—the renovated house or the newly-built flats—also enters into this, for it is the true financial return on your efforts. It is on the prevailing local prices for homes comparable in size and facilities to those which you will be offering for sale which this figure will depend.

To summarise the above, the following are the parameters to decide if a particular house is a suitable purchase for renovation (or conversion):

1. *What is the lowest price you can buy for?*
The best bet first time round is a small property suitable for conversion into two or three units.

2. *How much will the work cost?*

3. *How much will you have to pay in fees to:*
    (a) Solicitors (for negotiating the purchase and resale and conveyancing the property—see Chapter 5).
    (b) Estate agents (for selling the property if you cannot sell it by other means).
    (c) Surveyors (for surveying the property purchased and possibly others which the surveys proved unsuitable).
    (d) Architects for drawing up plans, and obtaining planning permission. (If you are not prepared to do this yourself).

Remember that (a), (c) and (d) might be involved on more than one property—ie, failed attempts to purchase.

4. *How much interest will you have to pay on loans,* ie, how long will it take to complete the work *and sell* the property?

Also, does a partner expect a minimum return on his capital? If so add it to this figure.

5. *How much can you* realistically *expect to sell for?* To get the answer, subtract 1, 2, 3, and 4 from 5.

The figure left is your profit. Is it enough for you, bearing in mind the amount of your time which the project will take up?

If there is *no* profit to be had on the basis of your calculations with the above system, the project may still be worth doing if you intend to undertake a considerable part of the work yourself, as you will pay yourself a wage out of category 2, the funds allocated to the work.

Above all, you must allow a reasonable amount of leeway in 5 for the house to stand on the market unsold for some time, particularly if it will not be completed in the spring or early summer, which is when most purchases are made. Even properties with everything going for them can be quirky in this respect.

If the property you intend to purchase passes these tests with flying colours then you are in business in no uncertain terms!

Change of use and planning permission

Some properties on the market may already have permission from the local authority for a 'change of use', and planning permission for conversion into flats. This will probably have been obtained by the vendor to make selling easier, or maybe he had intended to convert himself and changed his mind. If you decide to buy one of these houses there need be no delays to prevent you starting work once you are the owner.

Where this is not the case, the agent should be able to tell you if an application for permission stands a good chance of being well received by the council or corporation. This usually depends on housing policy for the area. Some areas are kept strictly to single-dwelling properties. Houses in others where there has already been a degree of 'multiple occupation', ie, conversion of single dwellings into flats, are generally allowed to be divided up. They are granted change of use as a matter of course.

In any event, whatever the agent says, if you are very interested in the property, contact your local authority to find out from the horse's mouth if they are likely, not only to grant change of use, but more specifically, agree to the kind of layout which you propose to feature in the property. By this method you can find out as near as is humanly possible *before* you send in a formal request for planning permission whether it is likely to be accepted or not.

At this stage it is advisable not to trust *anyone* completely. Keep asking questions until you are satisfied either that plans exist and have formally been approved (ask the estate agent to show them to you and if doubtful get an architect to check if the layout is workable), or that the council is amenable to your intentions. At this stage comes the largest element of risk in the project: at some point you have to take a blind leap, and this is it.

Once as reassured as you can be on this score, you must acknowledge that to some extent the granting of these permissions is in the lap of the gods. It is very seldom practical to go any further with the matter at this stage of the proceedings; a formal submission for planning permission may require as many as eight or

41

nine copies of detailed plans and proposals to be prepared and sent to the local authority for scrutiny. The
whole process, from preparation of the plans through
to the decision by the authority whether to give con-
sent, can take three or four months, or even longer.
All the more reason to check if the way seems clear
before you start to apply formally, and especially
before you buy the property. But, if you are as sure as
you can be of the acceptability from the planning
angle, and with your budget calculated, the house you
have chosen is a good candidate for your renovation.

Properties not needing change of use or
planning permission
If you decide to plump for renovating rather than converting into flats, and the house has been used as one
dwelling only, it will not be subject to change of use or
planning permission. This, of course, also applies to
properties already in use as flats at the time of purchase (you may intend to revamp a house with this
layout, and simply modernise and improve the existing flat units in it). However, there is less potential for
profit with these types of scheme than with converting a house into flats, so it's six of one . . .

Assuming you have raised your funds by this
stage, all that remains to be done is to go ahead with
the standard procedures which anyone buying
property is subject to. These are:

1. Having the property surveyed
2. Having the property conveyanced
3. Making an offer in order to purchase the
property.

These items are dealt with in Chapter 4.

Planning permission: some details of the procedure

The place to contact is the Planning Department of
the local authority; ask what is needed.

1. Change of use

If converting from house to flats, this is relatively simple: the answer is 'yes' or 'no'. If the answer is 'yes':

2. Submit the application for planning permission

This will consist of architect's drawings of the new layout, showing plan views of each floor of the building, and elevation views of any relevant external aspects (front and rear of the property, and the sides if altered), and in some cases a plan view of the roof layout.

Items shown should be:

(a) Structural alterations, eg opened-up walls, with details of arrangements for supporting the weight of the structure over the new opening, ie rolled steel joists etc.

(b) New plumbing, drainage over and below ground, ventilation, insulation, sizes of new doors and windows.

Your local authority planning department will farm out copies of the plans to various departments (you will have to supply them with sufficient numbers). These will include copies to:

The District or Borough Surveyor. He will deal with (a) above, and will be interested in lintel sizes, wall loadings and specifications for concrete mixes. He will also be the official who comes to see if the property conforms with the fire regulations when the work is done. (The 'DS', as he is called, is also a very helpful informal source of advice on site during the job, for his experience has made him aware of the difficulties involved in translating drawings into reality.)

The Environmental Health Officer. He will check that the items in (b) are acceptable.

The Grants Officer (usually, in practice, a Health Officer). Sometimes you will have to ask specifically if the proposals are eligible for a grant, sometimes you will be told as a matter of course.

Other departments, eg Historic Buildings. If the building has been classified by this department as being of historic interest, there may be restrictions upon what you can do to it. These apply mainly to the exterior of the property.

The planning permission saga can be a long and tedious business. The only way you can sidestep it with no risk is if you are just carrying out a straightforward refurbishing job on a single dwelling. Even so, you will be obliged to send details of structural alterations to the DS and plans of any but the most minor changes in drainage to the Health Officer.

Once over this hurdle, it's a relief to find that the people behind these titles are very often easy to work with and not lacking a sense of humour; there are, of course, exceptions . . .

It is possible to prepare the plans yourself if you are so inclined. Try to familiarise yourself with the conventions and symbols used by architects in plans and written specifications of works which often accompany them (the Penguin *Dictionary of Building* is useful here). While drawing plans you can also mark in the positions of electrical points, lights and switches, radiators and gas fires, consumer units (or fuse boxes), and gas and electricity mains and meters. None of these need be shown for local authority purposes, but they are of tremendous assistance in planning and carrying out the work.

Chapter 4
Buying the Property

Once you have decided that the house is a viable proposition for your purposes and have satisfied yourself by carrying out preliminary enquiries as outlined in Chapter 3, you should put in an offer on the most suitable property available. You are still relatively uncommitted to anything at this stage.

The sequence of events

Make your offer:

1. *Subject to contract,* and
2. *Subject to survey.*

Number 1 keeps you off the hook until the vendor starts getting serious and the drafting of contracts takes place, at which point it starts getting progressively more difficult (though by no means impossible) to back out of the deal.

Number 2 protects you against having to break your neck rushing around organising surveys on every property you may be keen enough on to make a potentially binding offer for, or at least cause bad feeling in the vendor's camp if you backed out.

You are not obliged to have a survey carried out at all. You must choose, depending on whether you have any knowledge of building construction and, if so, how much, between several alternatives.

(a) An all-the-stops-out survey, costing possibly £200 or more, will tell you far more than anyone would ever want to know about the building.

The overly pessimistic tone of these documents would be enough to convince the uninitiated that no house is ever fit to be lived in, but

45

with this kind you are paying for the fine-tooth comb approach, and that's what you get.

(b) The other extreme is to cast a weather eye over the edifice and draw your own conclusions. Of course this is all right only if you have considerable experience.

But if you don't want to kiss goodbye to the sort of money needed for an extensive survey, there is now a 'mini-survey' at a fraction of the cost, which will tell you all you need to know about potential weak points, hazards, and shortcomings in the structure itself without telling you if there is a draught under the kitchen door and so on.

If the survey comes out well, whatever form it takes, you next need to have the local authority search carried out. This is a check on the legalities connected with the property in the same way as the survey is a check on its structural soundness. You can make your offer:

3. *Subject to search*, in the same way as you made it subject to factors 1 and 2. At this stage, the only tangible form of commitment to the property you will have to make is to fork out a:

4. *Stakeholder's deposit.* This is a nominal sum which shows willing and reinforces the 'gentlemen's agreement' which is still all that exists between you and the vendor to prove that your interest in the property is genuine and not just an offbeat way of passing the time. Once

5. *The survey* (or similar) has been carried out, if you are still interested in the property and

6. *The offer is accepted*

7. *The local authority search* must be commenced. This is where your solicitor really gets to work. Up till now the only involvement he may have had with the transaction will have been in the formal confirmation of the offer with the vendor's solicitor. The survey is your responsibility, but he will now commence the checks on the status of the property. This involves:

(a) Checking there are no compulsory purchase orders on the property—your house could be in the path of a proposed new motorway, and as such capable of being forcibly 'purchased' from you by the local authority at a fraction of its true value.

(b) Ensuring that there is no order for demolition or expensive repairs imposed by the Environmental Health Department. Either would cost you dearly.

(c) Checking the deeds of the property. They will show if the person you have offered to buy from is really the owner of the property. They will also show boundary demarcations with adjacent properties etc.

All of these checks come under the general title of:

8. *Conveyancing*. You can do this yourself if you wish (see reading list on page 131) but a good solicitor will take care of it all and you need then only involve yourself when he refers to you details which he thinks you should know about.

If all is well you can press on to the next stage:

9. *Drawing up the contracts*. You and the vendor each have a contract drawn up for you by your own solicitor. These are then exchanged and signed by the other party (still supervised by the solicitors).

10. *Exchange of contracts* has then taken place, and this is the stage at which you start parting with bigger funds—usually 10 per cent of the purchase price of your house.

Within a statutory time limit, usually around four weeks,

11. *Completion* must take place. At this stage the transaction is complete; the keys are handed over to you and the remaining 90 per cent (minus shareholder's deposit) is paid to the vendor. You are now:

12. *The new owner.*

Sources of properties

1. Estate agents

In discussing the typical sequence of events in a purchase, the above example deals with a property advertised through an estate agent. The premises would have been offered for sale at a fixed rate, around which offers would be based. Although you may have got to know more about property generally by your 'tour' of their offices (see Chapter 3) you do not necessarily have to buy from an estate agent.

2. Private purchase

If you should get to hear through the grapevine that a house is being put up for sale, you can contact the vendor and buy from him directly. This cuts out the expense of the estate agent's fee (usually 2 to 3 per cent of the purchase price). As you will have saved the vendor this expense, you can ask him to reduce this price a little accordingly.

3. Auctions

Usually conducted by estate agents, auctions *can* be a useful means of buying. You will have to look extremely carefully for bargains if you attempt to purchase this way.

Properties offered for sale by auction are usually in such rough condition that it is impossible to get a building society mortgage for them, hence they are seldom offered at a fixed price in the agent's office window because they will be taking up valuable space which could be used for more saleable properties. They are only viable propositions for builders, renovators and others who can raise ready cash to buy them and devote considerable time, effort and resources to refurbishing.

There are bargains to be had here, but be careful. It's easy to get carried away in the excitement of the auction room, and the longer the bidding goes on the more it seems the house must be worth. Here are a few tips on how to proceed:

(a) *The auction programme.* This is available from the estate agent or auctioneer some time before the auction. Get a copy. If there are any properties which interest you, quiz the agent about them at this stage while you still have enough time to sort yourself out. The last few precious days before the auction will slip away like seconds.

(b) *Maximum bid for each property.* You must try to estimate the costs involved on each potential purchase, ie buying, converting, etc. Fix a cut-off point for each house on which you propose to bid—your maximum offer. This may be a different figure for different properties, as some will be larger than others and will require more work, even though they will eventually bring a greater return on resale. Others may be more expensive but need less work done, thus involving the same total outlay.

Profitability of the project is the bottom line, remember, so once the bidding has reached your cut-off point, drop out or face unpleasant consequences later.

(c) *Securing a purchase in the auction room.* If your bid is accepted, things start to happen much faster in the auction room than in a transaction through an estate agent. The contract of sale is drawn up on the back of the auction catalogue and you will be required to put pen to paper at this stage, which is equivalent to exchange of contracts in the other method of purchase.

You will almost certainly be expected to hand over 10 per cent of the purchase money in ready cash at this stage. (This brings back fond memories of sitting with £4000 in one's pocket for a whole afternoon!) The balance of payment must usually be made within a set period from the date of the auction. This is about two weeks as a rule.

As with the other kind of purchase—see 1—if you do not pay the balance within this period you may forfeit your deposit, although if the vendor's camp feels that there are unavoidable delays and that the money will eventually be forthcoming, this 'completion date' can be extended.

4. Sealed bids
Sometimes a different form of bidding is used: each bidder writes down one bid — the highest he thinks he will need to outbid the opposition — and seals it in an envelope. The bidders are called to a special meeting by the auctioneer, at which the bids are opened in full view. The highest bid secures the property.

The most obvious feature about this kind of sale is that each bidder is completely in the dark about how much his competitors have bid. This has both a good and a bad side; there is no risk of bidding more than you intend in the heat of the moment, which could happen in the auction room, but as you only have one shot you must take care not to bid too low. Where sealed bidding is used you will be told the reserve price — the minimum figure the vendor is prepared to sell for — by the estate agent beforehand. (If only two or three bidders are involved, all concerned will not want to waste time on the exercise because everyone has put in too low a bid to effect a purchase.)

Often sealed bidding is used for properties which have been withdrawn from open auction after failing to reach their reserve price. This means that if you were at the open auction you will have had a chance to check out the opposition during the bidding there. This can be followed up by a chat to the estate agent where you may get more clues as to your chances of successfully clinching a sale.

Summary of methods of purchase

1. By far the commonest form of house purchase is through estate agents by means of an offer made to the vendor via the agent. The property will be on the agent's books at a set asking price.

Remember — you do not have to offer the asking price. Even with the cheapest premises you should make an offer which is at least £2000 lower, or thereabouts. This is irrespective of other factors such as a grossly unrealistic asking price, or any features which make it seem a gift. The vendor will almost certainly be asking more than he expects to get—it's one of the silly money games in the property business, but you have to go along with it.

2. The private purchase—the best if you can find one.

3. The auction—more tricky than the other two types. It's not a good idea to attempt an auction purchase for your first project.

Chapter 5
Two Typical Projects

In this chapter we have taken examples of two types of property commonly encountered during the course of renovation work.

The first is a house suitable for conversion into two flats. It is a medium-sized three-storey property converting into a one-bedroom basement flat and a two-bedroom maisonette.

As explained in Chapter 1, the property must be suitable for conversion without too much alteration. Ideally, it should have two separate entrances (one for each proposed flat); say, for example, a main front door to the ground floor and a side entrance to the basement. This arrangement means that you have only to remove the staircase to the basement and seal off the resulting gap to make the basic separation into two units, and it will have been achieved without a lot of structural work.

Converting into two flats means, of course, that you will have to install two of everything—kitchens, bathrooms, gas meters, water tanks, and so on—and when you sell, two lots of solicitor's fees. You will also need planning permission because you intend to 'change the use' of the property. However, having said that, the profits are nearly always higher when converting property into flats, and this type of property is ideal for a first conversion.

Conversion of a three-storey house into two flats

Here is a typical breakdown of the work involved in this conversion:

	£
Purchase of property	32,500
Fees etc (solicitors, stamp duty, telephone, District Surveyor, excluding estate agent)	800
Separation into two units	300
Two bathrooms	2,000
Two kitchens	2,000
Two electrical installations	1,700
Extension to basement flat	1,000
Roof work	900
Plastering/external render	500
Damp-proof course	600
Drainage/plumbing	900
Gas supplies	100
Two central heating installations	2,000
Painting/decorating	1,000
Carpentry	800
Scaffolding	400
Garden	500
Contingencies	1,000
Total expenditure	49,000
Profit	26,000
Sale of two flats	75,000

The second example is a small three-storey house, unsuitable for conversion into flats (due to its size), but ideal for renovation as a two-bedroom family town house.

The criteria for selecting this type of property have already been discussed, so we won't go into them again except to say that planning permission for 'change of use' will not normally be required as you will not be changing the way in which the house was designed to be used.

Renovation will usually be cheaper and quicker than conversion, but again, profits could be lower and your prospective buyers will be more particular.

Renovation of a house as a single dwelling

Here is a typical breakdown of the work involved in this renovation:

	£
Purchase of property	46,500
Fees etc (solicitors, stamp duty, telephone, District Surveyor, excluding estate agent)	1,000
Bathroom	1,000
Kitchen	1,800
Electrical installation	1,400
Roof work	1,400
Plastering/external render	2,800
Damp-proof course	800
Drainage/plumbing	1,500
Gas supply	300
Central heating	1,900
Painting/decorating	1,700
Carpentry	1,800
Scaffolding	800
Garden, rubbish clearance	700
Contingencies	1,000
Total expenditure	19,900
Profit	23,600
Sale of property	90,000

As can be seen, most of the items are the same in both examples, except that in the conversion into flats it was necessary to build a single-storey extension on to the basement flat to provide a bathroom. Even though building an extension can be an expensive item, the greater profit to be made from the sale of two flats (as opposed to one house) makes it easily affordable.

It will obviously take longer to do the conversion project than it will the renovation and any borrowed money will be tied up for longer. So the quicker and more efficient you are, the bigger will be your profits.

When designing your layout for a conversion into flats, try to keep as many of the services as possible confined to each flat. In other words, as an example, put separate cold water tanks in each flat rather than putting them all in the main loft. This will avoid the problem of residents having to go through each other's flats when they want to maintain or service their systems. It also makes installation cheaper because pipe work does not have to be run so far.

The same applies to electrical work. Try and keep consumer units (fuse boxes) within the relevant flat, rather than bunching them all together in a hall cupboard.

Separating items like this will ensure that each flat is properly self-contained, something which prospective buyers will appreciate.

Chapter 6
Professional Advice

Once you embark on a project of this nature, it is worth getting all the advice you can. If you know anyone who has done some work on their own home, even if what they have done seems trivial in comparison to the size of the project you intend to undertake, the knowledge they have gained will be valuable to you. It is often the small details and less important items that tend to get overlooked when tackling a large job.

Banks

Whether or not you are raising money from the bank, your bank manager is an excellent source of down-to-earth advice on money matters and business schemes generally. If you do intend to borrow from the bank, he will want to see details of your scheme, including:

1. Total investment—yours and any other person's involved
2. Cost of the property you intend to buy
3. The total cost of renovation, including solicitors' and estate agents' fees, and bank interest
4. A detailed breakdown of how the money will be spent, as described in the specimen sheet in Chapter 5
5. How long the work will take (be realistic).

The more detail you present to your bank manager, the more impressed he will be with your organising ability, and the more detailed his advice will be. He may also want to have a look at the property you intend to buy.

Solicitors and accountants

Your solicitor, if you have chosen him carefully, will provide you with information on company law, conveyancing, auctions and legal requirements generally. His advice is not free, of course, but as you will undoubtedly have to consult him anyway, you might as well cover as much ground as you can in one visit.

Another invaluable source of professional advice is an accountant. As with solicitors, try to choose one who is used to dealing with small businesses and perhaps has some knowledge of property companies. He can advise on self-employment; company law (if you intend to form a company); your tax position in respect of income tax, capital gains tax, corporation tax and PAYE. It is absolutely essential to sort out your tax position and possible liabilities before you set up your business and start any actual work.

As your accountant will be the one who looks at what you have spent and how you have spent it on an annual basis, he will be able to offer advice from time to time on how you are shaping up as a property dealer.

Architects

At some point you will need drawings of your proposed renovation (for local authorities etc). Apart from supplying you with professional drawings, the architect will be in the position to offer advice on what he thinks will work in a practical sense in your property and, of course, what won't work. If he is used to designing layouts for domestic properties, he will be aware of the most detailed aspects of house renovation.

Free advice

There are plenty of sources of free professional advice. It may seem to you that you will become confused by taking advice from every possible quarter, but it is worthwhile taking it all in and then evaluating what is going to be useful now and what perhaps will help you later on.

The following are particularly useful:

1. *Estate agents.* They can help enormously by advising on property values in a particular area. They can tell you what sort of price you should pay for the property you are considering and what sort of price you should expect to get after your renovation. They have their fingers right on the property pulse and can tell you which type of property (eg, flats or bed-sits) is more in demand, and will therefore sell quickly, in a particular area. They are keen to advise because you may be buying your property from them initially, and you may be selling the finished product through them. Their advice on how to set out your conversion (where to put kitchens, bathrooms etc) is also worth having. You can even get a cross-section of ideas from several agents.

2. *Inland Revenue.* Your local tax office will supply you with booklets and leaflets on any taxes you are likely to encounter, and on PAYE, and on how to employ sub-contractors. You will need to approach them anyway if you intend to become self-employed.

3. *VAT office* (listed in telephone directories under 'Customs and Excise'). They will supply you with information and booklets about what you can claim, should you be eligible for registration. The benefits of registration were that you could claim back some or all of the VAT spent during the course of renovation, but these were removed in the 1984 Budget and it may be difficult to register, as a property company.

4. *Insurance brokers.* They will advise on types of insurance that you will need in the course of buying and working on your property and, of course, will sell you the policies as well.

5. *Local councils.* The town hall is a mine of information to someone renovating property. During the course of renovation you will become involved with the local authority departments, so it will be of benefit to you to go and see them before you start planning your first conversion/renovation, or making work schedules.

They will assess whether you are eligible for any grants and will advise on fire regulations, drainage, and anything else relevant to their interest in your property. In our experience they have always been extremely helpful.

6. *Materials suppliers*. Visit large builders' merchants and specialised suppliers, and collect price-lists and information sheets on the products that you are likely to use. Also make notes of who sells what and whether materials are regularly in stock or have to be ordered. Check on whether suppliers will deliver reliably, as waiting for materials can cause irritating delays to your carefully planned work schedule.

The large builders' merchants can also advise on the suitability of particular materials, but whether or not you use them depends on whether there are good cheaper alternatives. It is up to you to check on prices and quality, as buying sensibly is crucial to making your expected profit on the finished job. Deciding whose advice to take isn't always easy. Generally, the more efficient the firm, the sounder the advice.

7. *Other sources*. Friends who are architects or surveyors; friends who are builders and can offer practical advice; anyone you know who already runs his or her own business and can give advice on day-to-day running and control.

Chapter 7
Employing Others

In starting up a business of this nature from scratch it is unlikely that you will want to become involved in employing full-time staff. It would, in fact, be unwise to do so, because you will not be in a position to offer permanent, continuous employment by renovating one house at a time. Should you eventually progress to being able to buy and renovate several houses at the same time, it might be worth considering, but there are still drawbacks.

If you take on people as employees you will need to give them a contract of employment, provide sickness/accident and holiday pay, and pay employers' National Insurance contributions. You will also have to operate a PAYE tax scheme. Obviously, this would be time-consuming and expensive. So for this type of business it is much better to employ contractors and/or casual labour.

Contractors

A contractor can be a builder, who will carry out some or all of the work, or a specialist tradesman—electrician, plasterer, carpenter etc.

One advantage of using a contractor is that he will price the job (usually free of charge) for a fixed amount. This means that, barring a few possible extras, you will know before you start exactly what the work will cost. Another advantage of using contractors, rather than doing the work yourself, is that the quality of the work should be better. It will also get finished more quickly.

Having raised these points, it is necessary to say that there are good and bad contractors, and you should always try to use people who have been recom-

61

mended, or who you have previously used yourself. If this is not possible, then try to look at some of the work they have done on other houses, and assess for yourself how good they are. Genuine builders and contractors won't mind you looking at examples of their work.

It is a good idea to get at least three quotes for any job you intend to contract out.

If you employ a builder to do most or all of the work, he then has the status of main contractor and it is quite likely that he will employ specialist trades himself. These specialists would then be sub-contractors to the builder and as such would be answerable only to him. Therefore, it is up to you to keep an eye on the quality and progress of work and take up problems as they arise with the builder himself.

Alternatively, you can act as the main contractor yourself, and bring in specialist trades as you need them.

The best way to get contractors to quote for a job is to supply them with drawings and a detailed specification. There is then no question of confusion over where things go and what should be done.

If you do intend to do the work yourself, you may employ help in the form of casual labour. Casual labour means exactly that. You employ people, generally unskilled, to work on your job a day or a week at a time without contract, and for an agreed labour figure only. This can be very useful, especially in the early stages of the job, when there is a lot of demolition and rubbish clearing to do. Also at the end of the job when there is clearing up, gardening and cleaning to do.

Supervision

Supervising the work as it proceeds is all-important in getting the results you want from the finished job. If you are going to run the site yourself you will be kept busy and you will have to be on your toes.

Once you have selected your contractors and accepted their quotes, you must arrange start dates. Try and keep to your programme (Chapter 9). Ask contractors for start dates in writing. They should be able to start within a few days of the date they give.

Try to arrange things so that there are not too many people working on the site at one time, especially if it is a small house. People get in each other's way and quality suffers. Also, if you are running things, it is important to establish who is buying materials and hiring plant/tools etc. If it is down to you, it is important to check on availability and delivery, and to get any materials on site before the work-force arrives, because they will want to start work immediately. If materials are not ready for them they will probably leave the site and you will then have to wait until it is convenient for them to fit you in again. An upset of this sort will then delay other contractors as well, so careful planning is very important.

If you are employing a builder to carry out all the work, then of course he will bring in sub-contractors at the appropriate time, and will probably want to supply materials as well. This will relieve you of a lot of planning and ordering, but is likely to cost you more, obviously.

Whether you run the site yourself or employ a builder, supervision by you is of paramount importance. You are the boss—it is your money that is being spent—and the people employed on the site are working for you. Don't get talked into taking short cuts just to make the builder's life easier. Do things the way you want to do them and in the way agreed in the quotes. This doesn't mean that there is no room at all for compromise. You will need a good working relationship with your builder, and you ought to be able to accept his advice on some matters, he probably having more practical experience than you.

If you are actually working on the site yourself then of course supervision is no problem; otherwise you should arrange a visit at least every other day (every day if you can manage it) to assess progress and sort out any problems that have arisen—and there will always be some. Contractors nearly always appreciate regular visits by their clients. Don't be afraid to point out things that are not to your liking. It is much easier to sort out problems as they occur, rather than when the whole job is finished.

When converting a house into flats, it is a good idea to try and finish one in advance of the others. This then acts as a show flat and you can put it on the market straight away. Should somebody be interested in buying, the deposit they put down could help your cash flow enormously.

Payment/Wages

Whether you form a company or partnership, or run the whole project on your own, you are treated as a contractor by the Inland Revenue.

This means that you are responsible for checking certain tax details before you employ people. If you employ contractors who are limited liability companies (they have the word 'Limited' after their name) or other corporate bodies, there is no special action required by you. Contractors who are not limited companies may or may not be holders of a tax exemption certificate. Those who are not, along with persons supplying casual labour, will involve you in more work. You will be required to deduct 30 per cent (currently) of all payments made to them, and to send those deducted payments regularly to the Inland Revenue. Your accountant can explain in detail.

Contractors who possess a current tax exemption certificate are required to show it to you, and you have to check that it is in order. You can then pay that contractor in full, without deduction of tax. The Inland Revenue issue pamphlets which explain the position in detail.

Once a contractor is on site (or even before) he will want some money. Most contractors ask for a deposit and then, depending on the length of the particular contract, further regular payments. These regular payments are known as stage payments because the money is paid in stages—weekly or monthly—in accordance with the amount of work done.

It is vital that you do not pay too much too soon. Assess the progress to date, with any extras, and agree a fair payment with the contractor bearing in mind that if he is supplying materials he will need more than someone supplying labour only.

Before making any final payment, make sure that everything has been done to the agreed specification, and that installations such as central heating, wiring etc actually work. It is in your own interest to make a list of any outstanding items, however small, and present it to the contractor before final payment.

Sometimes an agreement is made for retention of a portion of the contract sum for a set period, perhaps six months, to cover any faults that may occur, but this should be agreed before the contract is signed. Also make sure that guarantees are in order where applicable.

Casual employees are quite often paid daily in cash, but you must deduct tax and keep records.

Watching your renovation take shape is fascinating and rewarding, but the importance of supervision and site control cannot be over-stressed, nor can careful assessment of 'work done' before making payments.

Chapter 8
Running the Site

Settling down to your best method of working can take a little time, so it is best for you to spend some time on the site doing some of the preparatory work and generally getting the feel of working there. This familiarisation will help you when the major work starts to take place.

Daily operation

One of the first things to do is to produce a breakdown of the work to be undertaken. You should already have produced a schedule (Chapter 5) and have a rough idea of the time each section of the work will take. By combining the two you can produce a programme for use on site which will give you easy reference to the state of progress on the site at any time. It will also help you to plan the arrival of contractors.

Try and arrange things so that one job leads on to the next. For example, laying new drainage and a new manhole would then allow the complete installation and testing of internal plumbing and sanitary ware. The sequence of operations is important and you should spend time working it out properly.

Fix your programme on a sheet of card and hang it on the wall where you can easily and quickly refer to it.

Even if you are doing all the work yourself it is still worth having a programme.

You should also equip yourself with a site diary. Only by recording events daily can you run your project efficiently. It is often crucial to know, for example, when a contractor visited the site, or how many hours were worked on a particular day by some-

one you were paying by the hour. So record everything—it will pay dividends at the end of the job and
will serve as an invaluable reference book on sub-
sequent property conversions.

Site cleanliness

To make your site run well, it is necessary to keep it
clean and tidy. A daily sweep up keeps efficiency at a
peak. Bag up rubbish as it accumulates and store it
away from the working area. Arrange regular rubbish
collections, or hire a skip.

Storage

A common problem, especially in a small house, is
where to store materials. You can be sure that
wherever you store something large—that will be the
place you will need to work in.

You will always have to store some materials,
otherwise you will not be able to work at all, but as a
general rule never bring materials on to the site until
you intend to use them. Not only will they be in the
way, but they could get damaged or stolen. You will
also be paying for them before you have to.

Site security

Something often neglected while doing this sort of
work is security. You may enthusiastically smash out
an old door or window and then discover at the end of
the day that there is a large hole providing easy
access into your house straight from the pavement.
Anyone can then walk in and take your expensive
tools and materials, and it happens all the time.

Therefore, you should try and plan to do all the jobs
that will affect security of your property as early on in
the course of the project as is possible. By doing this
even if somebody breaks in there will be almost
nothing worth taking. New doors and windows come
into this category, and locks should be fitted as soon
as possible. Don't forget to seal up any temporary
means of access when you leave the site.

A typical programme for a small site is shown on
pages 70-71. The vertical column shows the various
items of work and can include the contractor's name.

The horizontal column shows the number of weeks that you expect the contract to run. Each box represents one week. All you have to do is to colour in the number of weeks you expect each item of work to take (based on the contractor's estimate), making sure that you space out certain sections of the work in order to avoid congestion on the site. It is obvious that preparation will come first and clearing the site will come last. It is also obvious that certain jobs can overlap—in fact they will have to, otherwise the job would never be finished in time.

A typical estimate and schedule of renovation including labour and materials

Item	Cost £	Time
Scaffolding/preparation	1,100	1 week
Structural brickwork	800	1½ weeks
Site telephone (including calls)	250	—
Supporting beams (steel work)	250	3 days
New windows	1,200	3 days
Damp-proof course/timber treatment	1,100	4 days
Remove old plaster work/timber	150	2 days
New roof and guttering	1,400	2 weeks
New electricity and gas supplies	500	3 days
Internal partition work	700	2 weeks
Electrical installation	1,500	2 weeks
Basement solid floor and tiles	900	2 weeks
New manhole/drainage	500	1 week
Internal doors/woodwork	1,600	2 weeks
Strengthen/repair front steps and cellar	300	3 days
External sand/cement render and repairs	800	1 week
Internal plastering	2,000	2 weeks
Plumbing—internal/external	700	1½ weeks
Central heating/hot water	1,800	1½ weeks
Kitchen and bathroom fixtures	1,600	2 weeks
Painting/decoration—internal/external	1,800	2 weeks
Garden/landscaping	500	1½ weeks

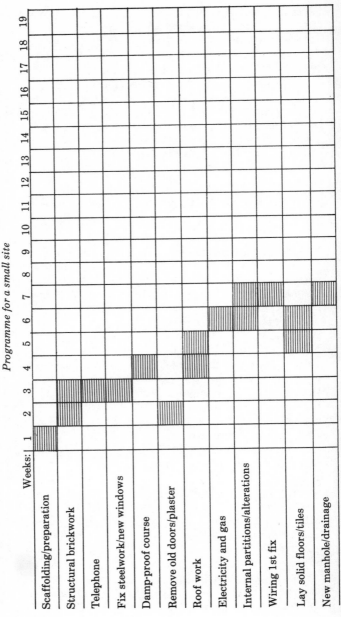

Programme for a small site

Weeks:	1	2	3	4	5	6	7	8	9	10	11	12	13	14	15	16	17	18	19
Scaffolding/preparation	▓																		
Structural brickwork		▓	▓																
Telephone			▓																
Fix steelwork/new windows				▓															
Damp-proof course																			
Remove old doors/plaster		▓																	
Roof work				▓	▓														
Electricity and gas						▓													
Internal partitions/alterations						▓	▓												
Wiring 1st fix							▓												
Lay solid floors/tiles						▓													
New manhole/drainage							▓												

Internal doors/woodwork

Strengthen and repair
front steps

External render/repairs

Internal plastering

External plumbing

Skirtings and
2nd fix woodwork

Central heating and
internal plumbing

Kitchen and bathroom
fitments

Wiring/electrical
2nd fix

Painting internal/external

Garden/landscaping

Carpets/cleaning

Clear site

Carpets	800	3 days
Skips/rubbish clearance	300	—
Cleaning/clearing site	150	2 days
Contingencies	1,000	—
Fees (solicitors/estate agents/etc)	2,500	—

The estimate and schedule lists the main items you are likely to encounter when carrying out a renovation. The amounts and the times quoted for each item will naturally be different when applied to different sizes and types of property and act only as a very rough guide here. However, this is the sort of list you should prepare (in more detail if you like) when doing your initial planning and costing. It is from this list that you make up your works programme. It is also the sort of detail that your bank manager and/or backers will want to see, so you should try to be as accurate as possible without trimming it too finely.

Buying materials and hiring equipment

Having materials delivered v. collecting them yourself
If you shop around the wide range of builders' merchants and timber yards, you will find that the prices and quality of the goods for sale vary quite dramatically. So does the service. You can spend three or four hours running round trying to find a particular item from several shops giving poor service, queuing for 30 to 45 minutes in each shop, while in that space of time another will have taken your order by phone and delivered the goods to the site. Deliveries can be a time saver. Instead of wasting a whole morning getting tired and irritated you will have been able to use that time by working on the site or doing something else productive.

Free deliveries
Free deliveries are the rule rather than the exception, so there is a double incentive to use them.

Same day deliveries
For every type of supplies you need there is usually at

least one merchant, particularly in the bigger towns and cities, who is much more efficient, helpful, and sometimes even cheaper than the others. You may well find that one of your suppliers can provide all of your materials and fittings for the entire job, ranging from sand and cement through to wooden mouldings and door furniture. Some places will take two or three days to deliver goods, and many will be reluctant to specify which day the delivery will arrive (problematic), but if you look around you will find the ones who will deliver the same day as the goods are ordered from them.

This has two positive advantages:

1. Same day deliveries avoid the risk of you (or your supplier) forgetting about making the necessary arrangements on the delivery date (ie, you to be there, him to load your supplies on to the truck on the right day)—it happens!

If you are involved with a lot of the work on the site, you will find that on some days there will be so many things happening at once that it is quite hard to remember everything (the surveyor and the health officers are guaranteed to turn up just when the phone starts to ring, and at the time you will probably be standing on one leg, holding up a half-hundred-weight concrete lintel and trying to carry out measurements accurate to one-eighth of an inch). If something crops up which forces you to leave the site it's much easier to forget about an impending delivery arranged two days ago than one arranged only hours before. This may seem a small detail, but it's all the little things like this which can collectively become a major headache if not organised to minimise unnecessary frustration.

2. In our experience, the companies who are prepared to deliver on the same day as the order is placed with them tend to be more friendly and cooperative, as well as more efficient. They have usually gone out of their way to make themselves that efficient, and are very often smaller firms who are on the up and up because of their go-ahead attitude.

Many of the older-established bigger firms in the

building trade, though not all, are hidebound by outdated working procedures and bored, unenthusiastic employees. In contrast to these dinosaurs are the new do-it-yourself supermarkets where most of the goods are on display and easily found by the customer; however, you must weigh against this the fact that they do not usually deliver goods and tend to be better for finished items, but rather pricey and inadequate for general items (see lists in appendix).

Hiring tools and equipment

Almost any of the tools and equipment needed on the building site can be hired. Apart from the most basic toolkit, eg electric drill, screwdrivers, hammers, bolsters, saws, tape measures, trowels, it is cheaper to hire than buy—you may only need some of them for a week at a time. You also save on the large quantity of storage space needed for stowage if you owned them all. Breakdowns can be less of a problem too—a replacement, at no extra cost, can be provided if equipment breaks down through no fault of your own, whereas having your own gear repaired or replaced causes either long delays or undue expense. Tools and equipment can also be delivered to the site.

Running the site office

You will need a site office of some description. Try to choose a room where the least work will take place, and equip it with a desk or table with a drawer and facilities for tea-making. If possible, you should also get a telephone. Ordering materials and hiring plant is made much easier if it can be done readily and quickly. It also enables others to contact you without delay—this may sound rather obvious but regular contact is important when running a business.

When asking for an installation, remember that a business telephone can be obtained more quickly than a private one.

In your drawer in the site office you should keep receipts, accounts, drawings and any other paperwork relating to the daily running of the site. All nonessential paperwork is better kept elsewhere to avoid clutter.

An important part of the daily running of the site is keeping accounts and records. You need to record all expenditure, including payments for materials, payments for work done by others and, of course, payments to yourself. It is worth making a record of transactions as they occur, even though you may be covered in mud at the time. Your accountant will want to see these records at some point, and they are particularly important if you have formed a limited company.

The more efficiently you run your site, the more smoothly the job will run, and others will respect your efficiency.

An office off the site

If you are fortunate enough to have the use of an office away from the site, maybe a spare room at home, you can equip it to a higher standard.

For a start, a typewriter is a major asset. Official letters always look better when typewritten, especially if you are using headed paper. A lot of confusion can be avoided by typing orders for materials, especially if your handwriting is a scrawl. A double order of kitchen equipment won't help your bank balance at all.

Always make sure that you have a spare cheque book in your office. There are few things more embarrassing than taking delivery of long-awaited supplies only to find that you have just used your last cheque for something else. Your materials will not be off-loaded, contractors and work will be held up, and you will have to arrange a temporary cheque book from your bank.

File all bank statements, planning approvals and letters. Make photocopies (or carbon copies) of any letters that you send, and file these. File contractors' invoices, tax deduction cards and books, and in fact everything relating to the business which you don't need to keep on site. Card files are adequate, but if you can get a proper filing cabinet—all the better.

Deal promptly with letters, especially to local authority departments, gas and electricity boards etc, otherwise they will lose interest in you and your project will be delayed. The Inland Revenue are also quite keen on prompt replies.

All financial transactions should be made from a bank account opened for business use only. This ensures that your personal money does not become involved and makes record-keeping much simpler.

It is unlikely that your office away from the site will need to be permanently manned. You won't need a full-time secretary, and incoming phone calls will be few and far between. However, there will be occasions when people need to get in touch with you. For this purpose it might be worth installing a telephone answering machine. It is only worth having one of these in your permanent office: on a building site it would soon be damaged.

Don't be tempted to spend too much time in your office, surveying your empire, as office work, although essential, is non-productive.

Keeping track of the finances

There will be some items which you will have to obtain yourself; it doesn't make sense to get a special delivery for the odd paintbrush or a bag of nails which you need *right now,* apart from the fact that even *asking* your friendly neighbourhood merchant is likely to go down like a lead balloon.

Cash kitty
You will have to keep a small cash float for these small items. £50 should be enough, although if you find that you regularly need more, don't practise the false economy of drawing so little out of your account at a time that you waste valuable hours standing in a long queue at the bank every other day to draw more.

However, a large quantity of loose cash on a building site can be a problem. Keep it in a separate wallet in your pocket as often as this is convenient, however much you trust your work-force; properties under-going repair are invariably easy to get into during the working day, and there are moments when there is no one around to keep an eye on valuables left near an open door.

Cheque book
Your cheque book will do most of the work for you in keeping your cash flow records tidy and organised. You can open accounts with your suppliers if you wish, but beware the temptation to ignore how quickly the monthly bill is mounting up just because you don't have to think about it when making each purchase—you could be in for a nasty surprise at the end of the month and if you or your supplier have got your sums wrong, nobody will be able to remember exactly what happened on the day in question. Paying for every purchase separately, on the other hand, enables you to check the goods while the transaction is still fresh in your mind, and you can fill in a separate cheque stub for each as an added precaution.

If you get to know your regular suppliers they will let you pay for the goods with quite large cheques (£500 or more) without any hassles over your creditworthiness. This can speed things up considerably.

Accounting procedures

We have already discussed the importance when obtaining your start-up funds, of impressing bank managers etc with costings and projections. It is also vital to keep certain records of the ongoing finances of the project. This side of things can become unnecessarily complicated if you listen to the armchair entrepreneurs who are all to ready to advise you about money matters, whether you want the advice or not.

Here are a few suggestions for keeping the simplest possible records:

Day-to-day accounting and keeping a record of cash flow
The simplest and sanest way to handle the accounting procedures of the company from day to day, whether you are running the operation as a sole trader

or through a limited company, is to keep three kinds of record:

1. *Cheque book stubs.* These should be filled in and preferably carry running totals of your bank balance on each; calculate it as each cheque is written, and you will have a means of cross-checking with your regular bank statements. If you *really* stick to a procedure of writing the amount of each cheque on the stub as you go along you will have a clear, easily evaluated record of your outgoings, for in addition to cheques for materials and labour, cheques written for petty cash will also be shown. This also applies to the paying in book; not many payments will be made into the account (apart from moneys from people buying your properties) but there will be the odd refund on goods returned etc. Remember it's these odd transactions which slip through the system, so be warned!

2. *All receipts for purchases.* All receipts for goods and services paid for should be kept in date order. Quite a simple arrangement will do—a metal spike on a stand as used in offices will ensure that most of the time the date order is kept except for the odd, forgotten rogue receipt.

3. *A cash book.* This must show, as a minimum, cheques cashed for use in the cash kitty, which you will find is indispensable—there is always a host of small items which cannot practically be paid for with a cheque, ranging from half a dozen nails to a replacement for a broken tea mug. Your cash book entry for each cash purchase will give a cross-check with their receipts.

Management of cash flow
The job must be kept on the move by the availability of ready cash throughout its duration. From the word go, when you ensure before starting work that the money you have gained access to will be enough to cover the works, interest, a contingency figure (to pay for unanticipated work, at least 10 per cent of the basic costing), solicitors, surveyors and estate agents, you must know at any time whether or not

you can afford to pay out more money on outstanding work to be done. Your budget must be adhered to.

Credit control must be practised. It is very difficult to reckon accurately how much you owe contractors if they are working on 'extras' which you have asked them to carry out, ie work which they have not estimated for but which turned out to be necessary when they finished the work which they *did* estimate for. Pressure of time often prevents an estimate being submitted — you will probably be very busy, and if the contractor has to stop working to draw up a costing he may not actually have time to do the additional work at once. He will probably have work arranged on other sites and may not be able to return to do the work for some time. Thus you may have arranged for these 'extras' to be done on a daily rate, ie you pay him an agreed sum for each extra day's work. If two or three contractors are undertaking this kind of work on your site, and you have been absentmindedly agreeing with their suggestions about work which they think necessary because you are so busy yourself, it's easy to run up an astronomical bill. So keep a weekly tally of these 'hidden' outgoings — they may not have to be paid until the work is completed but complacency will cost you dearly.

Additional accounting requirements for limited companies

If you are running your business as a limited company the requirements are more stringent than for the sole trader. As we have said, these are more than offset by the protections which limited liability provides.

You will be required to send the yearly returns to Companies House, showing the number of shares and shareholders in the company. You and your colleagues will probably be directors, as well as owners of the share capital, so these documents will show your current status within the company. The annual submission of these returns enables a check to be carried out on any changes in ownership of shares etc, and will be a mere formality in the early stages of the company's existence.

You will be required to produce annual company profit and loss accounts on a balance sheet which must be submitted to the Inland Revenue for scrutiny—your accountant will deal with all this, but remember that he will compile these documents from your own records (cheque book stubs, receipts and cash book), and you will have to pay him, so make his job as easy as possible.

Outgoings and income—some good points

One of the best features of buying and selling property and renovating it is that the book-keeping is simplified by the fact that income is not from a large number of sales of small items as in many self-employed businesses, but from a few sales of large items—flats and houses. Thus there is no problem with collecting unpaid debts, which can be a time-consuming and frustrating aspect of many business ventures.

Also, as you are managing the money yourself, how much of a wage you pay yourself, and when, are things which you can decide for yourself to some extent. However, the more you hold back on paying yourself the less bank interest you'll have to pay, and clearly if you exceed your allocation of wages in the early stages you will find it difficult to get back in step with it later. Again—be warned.

The most important aspects of finance and accounting

Consistent costing, estimating and budgeting before and during the operation are vital to the success of every project. However much flair for design you may have and however good a work force, if the finances get out of hand they can reach a point where profitability is no longer possible.

Chapter 9

The Work Itself—Some Practical Suggestions

So much for the organisation and management of your projects, but what of the actual nitty-gritty—the physical transformation of the property? Whether you are getting involved in any of the building work yourself or not, it is more than likely that you will be wondering what the most important do's and don'ts of a typical renovation/conversion are.

Although we do not intend to give a blow by blow account of all the practical aspects of the work, here are some general points: first you have to submit formal notice to the District Surveyor that you are about to start work. This is done on a standard form obtainable from his office.

Major items

There are several large items in an old, run-down property which will almost certainly need a major overhaul or complete replacement.

1. The roof

The roof will probably be suffering from several long-term leaks and the resultant damage and, in a house of 100 to 150 years old, it is worth considering re-roofing rather than patching up. A new roof, although not necessarily even seen by the prospective buyer of the property, is a good selling point. For instance, a new slate roof not only looks impressive on the surveyor's report (easily visible from the upper storeys of the house if on a single-storey rear extension, for instance), but the effectiveness of a patched slate roof is always extremely hard to judge (due to the means by which slates are fixed on the roof battens). The surveyor's eye can see at a glance if a new roof is weather-proof, hence he is much more likely to give it a clean bill of health. One of the problems with patching up is that the disturbances caused by the repairs can start new leaks in unreplaced sections; adjacent slates can get cracked when walked on, and flashings and soakers which have become porous over the years are prone to splitting.

We recommend that of any work which you decide to contract out, the roof should be given the most care. A good, reliable roofer will save a lot of aggro later in the job; leaks from a badly repaired roof have an unhappy knack of showing some time after completion of the work—tell-tale symptoms such as bubbling paint and crumbling plaster can be relied on to appear overnight just when you are about to show around a prospective buyer.

It will be useful to get the building weather-proof and give time for rain-damaged timbers and walls to dry out in the early stages of the project before some of the more delicate operations such as plastering, second fixings and decorating have to be carried out. Your roofer can be at work while you are getting the rest of the job moving. In fact he, along with the damp-coursing contractor, can be set to work as soon as the tracks have been cleared for starting the whole job (ie cash, and if necessary, planning permission and grants). If he is worth his salt he will be able to advise you on any structural work needed on the roof or if re-slating or re-tiling is sufficient. Leaks may have damaged the timbers, or old age might have caused them to sag.

A good way to check out your roofer if you have a slate roof is to observe his reaction to the suggestion that you should re-roof with tiles. This is a perfectly feasible thing to do, but tiles are much heavier than slates, and in almost all cases the roof would need to be strengthened to take the extra weight. If his answer takes this into account and he doesn't simply jump at the chance of making a quick buck by tiling on the existing timbers, it's a reasonable bet that he won't be the kind to take short cuts.

Don't be afraid to have a look at what he's doing up there from time to time; even if you don't understand it all, it shows you're concerned enough about the workmanship to keep tabs on even the most inaccessible parts of the property.

2. The damp coursing

This is the second most likely candidate for an outside contractor. The best companies give a guarantee, often of 25 years, for the work, and will deal with timber treatment for rot and woodworm at the same time. The quality of the service varies greatly between different companies. We recommend the companies mentioned in the appendix.

It is very handy to get the damp coursing done while the roofer is at work for the reasons mentioned in 1.

3. Solid floors

Any concrete or ceramic tiled flooring at ground level will have to be proven to be damp-proof to the satisfaction of the District Surveyor. In most cases, in this kind of property it will have been badly laid, or it will be uneven, worn and broken. You may well find the easiest thing to do is to pull the lot up, lay a concrete slab of 4 to 6 inches deep (consult the DS) on appropriate damp-proofing—pvc sheeting, or tanking of asphalt or similar material, and finish it all with a 2 inch screed of concrete. It usually costs as much to half do the job as to do the lot; if you need to mix more than 2 cubic metres of concrete, use ready-mixed—it is cheaper than mixing on site, much cleaner and less space-consuming (no lorry-loads of sand in the road for days, no bags of cement to 'go off' before usable), and much faster, sometimes a little too fast for comfort, in fact. You can get the delivery driver to pour it down a chute if, for example, you are flooring a basement, or if the site is not adjacent to the road, a pump can be provided by the firm supplying the concrete. Screeding can be done by hand-mixing or ready-mix, and should be done after the slab is dry enough to walk on and after any gas, water and electricity services have been laid on the surface of the main slab.

4. Heating
Gas central heating is by far the cheapest and most effective system available at present. It is a big selling point and refurbishing a house provides an excellent opportunity to install it. We strongly recommend it.

5. Electricity and water supplies
Again, half doing the job is usually as time-consuming as installing a completely new system; a partly rewired electrical system will only be as good as its weakest components, and that odd section of antique wiring you decide to keep because it's inaccessible and seems to be working all right will be the first to cause problems in the new system. As with other items, complete replacement gives you the opportunity to rationalise its layout and bring it all up to a uniform standard, which is just not possible if you try to patch up a system which has 'evolved' in a piecemeal fashion over decades of changing technology and building practice.

The same applies to the water supplies and plumbing, including water storage tanks.

6. Floors—the joists
Don't spend a lot of time and money ripping out floor joists wholesale just because a couple are rotten. Even if the floor is tilting it can be left as it is—most people are prepared to accept this as part of the charm of a period building. As long as the DS agrees that it presents or indicates no structural hazard to the building, any feature which would, in a new building, be criticised for being 'out of true' may well look more in keeping if it is slightly repaired at a jaunty angle rather than removed and rebuilt completely. The further you take the latter operation the more you run the risk of upsetting a sort of 'harmonious imbalance' that emanates from an old house in which walls have settled a little and doorways have moved.

It has been suggested by another writer that all the floors in a period property which is being converted should be pulled out and re-positioned to give equal headroom on each storey; instead of the original layout where, as the building is ascended, the ceilings become lower, the new floor positions would give ceilings of equal height on each floor, hence giving every unit adequate headroom. This is nonsense. The expense would be pointless. Apart from the inevitable loss of cornice mouldings on the lower floor(s), impressive ceiling heights of around 13 feet would vanish to make way for an average height of about 7 to 8 feet, with nothing accomplished; it is very rare, even in the top storey 'servants' quarters', to find impossibly low ceilings; often, low ceilings can be just as much of a selling point as tall, elegant rooms with ornate plasterwork. To the right buyer they can be more attractive, and dealt with imaginatively give a cheap opportunity to remodel the geometry of the top storey into interesting shapes. This is discussed in 7, but one final point against adjusting floor heights: the original windows will be at the wrong level. It might even not be possible to see out of the top floor windows at all unless you stood on a chair!

7. Ceilings
If the ceilings on the top floor of the main part of the house or of the extension are in bad shape, don't just replace them in the same layout as before. You have now a good opportunity to 'open up' the ceiling.

Often the rafters upon which the old ceiling was supported can be cut away, and a new ceiling fixed to the sloping rafters which support the external covering of the roof itself, the slates or tiles. The shapes which this can produce look very pleasing. They also effectively increase your room sizes (check that the proportions 'work' though—you may find that the resulting rooms will look too tall for their width) which makes the whole dwelling look more spacious than before.

The possibilities don't end there: you can install roof lights, which are small windows set in the roof itself. Apart from making an interesting feature in

85

the room they can be opened to give more ventilation as well as more light. A good point with roof lights is that they are now available cheaply — the smallest ones for as little as £30 each — from a variety of manufacturers. Most of them come with flashings and soakers and all the paraphernalia which used to make fitting them such a headache already attached. They are an outstanding bargain.

Your ceiling can be finished in plasterboard and plaster or the attractive and inexpensive alternative of tongued and grooved boarding, which is easy to fit and can be clear varnished or oiled to give the 'Scandinavian' look.

All these refinements need cost little more than a replacement for the wet, sagging ceiling which had to come out anyway. One word of warning — don't forget to put your wiring and insulation between the rafters first! The air space in the original loft will have provided a measure of insulation against heat loss. That cushion is effectively removed by opening up the ceilings, so you must compensate for it by increasing the new insulation accordingly.

Other important features

Here are some points on how to deal with other key aspects of the property:

1. Wooden floors
Some of the wooden floors in your house will be in very rough shape. It is notoriously difficult to find replacement floorboards which match the existing ones size for size — often each house of this age seems to have its own particular size of boards, while modern timber measuring systems use several different conventions, none of which comforms to the old sizes. There is also the difficulty of assessing sizes because of uneven wear.

The best solution to save you tearing your hair out by the handful and wasting time is to compromise with what you've got; settle for fully boarded floors (which can be sanded down and varnished) in some rooms, carpets, floor tiles or lino in others. This can be achieved by stealing boards from some rooms to provide ready-weathered, matching replacements for the missing and damaged boards in others. Kitchens and bathrooms, for instance, are excellent candidates for tiled or lino-covered floors. Pull up the old boards in these rooms and lay chipboard as a base for these finishes. This medium has a positive advantage over narrow floorboards in that it evens out differences in joist heights and gives a smoother surface on which to fit the tiles, as it has much fewer joints. Another plus is that inspection panels for plumbing checks and maintenance can be cut to exactly the required shapes and tiled over, with corresponding cut-outs in the tiling. This arrangement is virtually impossible with tiling on to floorboards, even if they are covered with hardboard first.

The age of the wood in the old floorboards gives them a rosy hue which is brought out by sanding and even more by each coat of varnish. Use a two-part varnish or sealant if you wish. We find that the better one-part polyurethanes (especially PU 15) are quite up to the job and less unpleasant to use.

2. The shell of the building

This item is likely to be too costly to tackle in the earlier projects, but if your costings for the work permit, and if the outward appearance of the building is particularly grim due to years of accumulated soot and dirt coupled with the ravages of an acidic atmosphere, it may be worth getting in a contractor to clean the stone or brickwork. The transformation is staggering; anyone who has seen the difference in the appearance of buildings such as the Albert Hall after cleaning will appreciate the truth in this argument. An amorphous browny-black blight on the landscape becomes transformed into a glowing work of art. The same is definitely true, in more modest terms, of many period houses which have been cleaned up.

The main things to remember about having the outside of the building cleaned are first, that it is expensive—at the time of writing a typical three-storey house 40 feet high by 34 feet deep by 24 feet wide will probably cost over £3000—and second, that the windows will have to be covered during the work to prevent the glass dissolving—one of the cleaning agents used is hydrofluoric acid, which has the distinction of being the *only* acid capable of doing this.

3. Architectural features

If your property has some interesting architectural features don't dispense with them: draw attention to them by restoration. Most of these decorative elements, usually but by no means only external, adorning various doors and windows etc, evolved over a long period of time and are carefully proportioned to please the eye. They are often crafted in sand and cement mortar (or 'plaster' to use the general term for outside and inside finishes of this kind). It can, however, be expensive to employ someone with the skills necessary to refurbish these features and, in addition, there is often more repairing to be done than meets the eye, for once disturbed they often crumble away to nothing and must be replaced completely.

Fortunately, there is now available a wide range of replacements for these mouldings which are fabricated in fibreglass so authentically that it is virtually impossible to tell the difference between the genuine article and the imitation. Unlike most of the original mouldings, they are not made up in situ, but factory-made and simply fitted in position with screws.

There are several advantages to this type of moulding:

First, they are light and easily fitted in position, whereas fitting those of the plaster variety not built in situ was and is a major operation due to their great weight.

Second, this reduces the number of people getting in each other's way on the site while fitting takes place.

Third, the quality of the workmanship is seen before the feature is installed—it can be soul-destroying, when your new plasterer has just rebuilt an important feature for you, to find that the result is not a great improvement on the original crumbling wreck. This may not be due to a lack of skill on the part of the plasterer, either; sometimes working conditions on the site can be difficult—if there has been a lot of rain (not an unfamiliar phenomenon in the British Isles) there may be several people who have been delayed by it bustling around making up for lost time, but getting in his way, or the rain itself may ruin a masterpiece before the plaster has enough time to cure.

There is also a wide range of pre-formed mouldings available for interior use. Being made from expanded polystyrene these are also light and easy to fit in position with the adhesives supplied by the manufacturers, several of whom are mentioned in the appendix.

It is always possible to re-run cornices or rebuild ceiling roses, either in plaster or substitutes, but you can easily end up spending a lot of money (invariably more than you thought) on these items. On your early projects try cleaning up the existing ones with water and a small brush. You may find that layers of distemper are hiding some pretty ornamentation. We discovered that a row of amorphous blobs on a cornice was in fact, after cleaning, an extremely delicate array of tudor roses moulded in plaster of Paris. A member of the local historic buildings department explained that careful brushing with water would enable them to be prised away from the cornice, brushed clean and refixed with cove cement, which is quick-setting and prevents you having to stand all day holding one moulding in place until it is secure.

4. Skirtings, door frames and architraves

Mouldings in wood present a similar problem to the renovator as to how much should be left and how much replaced. Many of the more elaborate skirting or wainscoting mouldings are irreplaceable if you are using ready-made off-the-peg styles, and having them made up by your local neighbourhood joiner is enough to induce palpitations of the cheque book. If you can't afford to do this, use the same arrangement as with the floors: collect together all the most exotic existing ones in the house and salvage the best-preserved sections; you can then use them to adorn the biggest, most ornately decorated rooms while fitting the more modest rooms with off-the-peg skirtings, of which there are some quite pleasant shapes available. One thing is for certain: nothing looks worse in a property which purports to have been 'renovated' than different styles of skirting board joined together on the same run of wall. Do it properly and the results will speak for themselves.

There is a slightly different but equally economical solution to revitalising tired door frames and the internal ornamentation on window frames. Most internal door frames consist simply of the 'lining', the 'door stop' and the 'architrave' moulding. Many renovators remove the lot and replace it all, but apart from the expense of all the new wood needed for this operation on all doors in the house, this is often unnecessary. It usually results in damage to the surrounding plaster, if not to the brickwork itself, which in turn can lead to a further 'infinite regress' of one job leading to another (an occupational hazard for the renovator), so nip it in the bud: the lining, which is simply a flat three-part frame (top and two sides), and which is there to hang the door itself on and to stop the walls from 'fraying', as it were, is invariably in sound condition except in the tattiest of properties. It is usually the architrave which gets the most battering. This is the almost invariably fluted moulding which overlaps the join between the lining and the edges of the plaster on the wall. If this is replaced with a new one, the transformation of the whole frame assembly is miraculous. The stop will probably need replacing as well—it will probably have been joined badly in several places—for it also gets fairly heavy wear and tear and it costs nothing to replace. The 'new architrave' method also works very well on window frames which look beyond the pale, particularly those which are set in panelling. The architrave is only nailed in position and can be carefully prised away from the frame assembly to make way for the new one.

Your local neighbourhood joiner will make up any specialised skirtings which you feel you cannot do without despite the expense.

5. Windows

When you are trying to save the pennies, windows present one of the biggest problems of all in renovating a period property. There is no satisfactory short cut when faced with a senile sliding sash window assembly—it's tempting to try and refurbish damaged glazing bars and fill gaps in the woodwork rather than replace the whole assembly, but when you work out just how much time you spend overall to get a very average result (on an old sash window it is virtually impossible to sand down paint-clogged woodwork to a smooth finish without horrendous expense) it's cheaper to have a new one made up. This despite the cost of at least £200 on a 4ft by 3ft assembly including costs of fitting sash cords and weights; the sizes are all different; almost every window in one of these houses is likely to have different dimensions from the others, and there may be several different glazing patterns (the layout of panes in the frames). Spending this much money may hurt but it pays off in the appearance and saves a lot of frustration and elbow grease at the painting stage, for the surfaced are satin smooth. A useful tip is to get your joiner (there is one near you—just look in the Yellow Pages) to paint them with primer before delivering. It may well be raining in the period after installation for some time before you can get around to doing it yourself, and once the woodwork is wet the sashes will jam due to swelling.

We much prefer, even when installing additional windows to a house, to use period-style windows in keeping with the age of the premises. This used to mean custom-building by the joiner, but some of the mass-producers of joinery, eg Magnet and Southerns, are expanding their ranges to include ready-made assemblies of this type, mainly Georgian so far. Their uses are limited as they are restricted to several specific sizes, which is, of course, how they can be so competitively priced. They may be useful where a new rear extension is being added to the property, for the available sizes can be 'designed into' the new work.

Suppliers of mass-produced joinery can be a cheap

source of plain sashes, ie simple frames which are set into the walls and glazed. They can be cut to different sizes easily. We have found them useful for forming inspection windows through which a row of gas and electricity meters installed behind them may be read; thus the meters can be read from outside the building without having to be fitted in bulky and ugly boxes on the outsides of the walls.

There is one position in the house where ready-made windows of a different style from those originally fitted may be used without a glaring visual clash, and that is in newly dug-out basements; these are seldom visible from the kind of distance where one tends to see the building as a whole. There are some excellent double-glazed units available with aluminium frames coated in unplasticised pvc with a white finish which makes painting unnecessary. Double glazing is more of a priority in a basement than in the rest of the house, which tends to be warmer anyway, and in this position advantage can again be taken of the opportunity to use off-the-peg sizes to cut costs. Companies of special note are mentioned at the back of the book.

6. Plastering
Many renovators replaster throughout from scratch. This is unnecessary. As long as plaster has not 'blown', ie become detached from the walls—probably due to damp, it is possible to put a smooth finishing coat of new plaster on top. Consult a good plasterer on this one—sometimes plaster, although still adhering well, may be crumbling due to sheer old age.

7. Fireplaces, fires and woodburning stoves
If your budget permits, it is well worth looking into the possibility of installing at least one period fireplace in each unit of accommodation. You may be lucky enough to have found a property to renovate or convert which has its original fireplaces intact or needing just a minimum of restoration. Stove black paint on the cast iron and a little quick-setting cement such as Prompt Cement or Jetcem around broken

marble and stonework will often suffice to bring a tatty, neglected specimen back to life. Don't waste time trying to repair a broken casting—it will never look as good as the original or a replacement, and it won't stand up to the heat of a fire. The same applies to broken fire-bricks which are difficult to match size for size with new ones.

Even if you are fitting central heating, it is worth considering going the whole hog and making the fireplace as much of a focal point in the room as it used to be, as a source of heat and the relaxing sight of flickering flames. Today's log effect gas fires look much more like a real log fire than their predecessors of the last 30 years or so; in fact, it's almost impossible to tell them from the genuine article. The heat output is only modest, however, and they are expensive to run, but what a perfect showpiece to help sell your property!

An alternative which has a double advantage over this system is to install a woodburning stove. First, rather than needing an ornate fire surround to set it off, which is the best setting for the log effect fires mentioned above, the woodburning stove is in many cases an ornate piece of furniture in its own right. You can use this to advantage—the fireplace need be no more than a rectangular opening at the base of the chimney breast, large enough to house the stove, or you can even stand it in front of the chimney breast. This works particularly well in combined kitchen-dining rooms where the slightly primitive appearance of the stove enhances the workmanlike feel of the surroundings. Fuel is easily available for these stoves even in the heart of the city so there is no problem with running them—building sites are a copious source of well-seasoned timber, and sawmills and woodyards produce a continual flow of unwanted offcuts which the proprietors will be pleased to see the back of. In fact, as a renovator you would have ready access to vast quantities of reject timber from your sites, so you might well want to install one in your own home.

The second advantage of the woodburning stove is the heat which it puts out—much more than an open fire. Some of the Norwegian Jotul stoves put out 9 to 16 kilowatts, which is as much as five double bar electric fires. Ash rarely has to be raked out as combustion is so efficient with the stove doors closed that the fuel is nearly all turned into heat. As a result no smoke is produced, so that these stoves may be used in smokeless zones.

If you are considering tackling a country cottage renovation or conversion these stoves are particularly practical. In many country areas there is no mains gas. This makes cheap central heating impossible—electricity is expensive, and bottled gas is too. A woodburning stove is easily installed in an existing chimney—it makes a beautiful feature of an old inglenook fireplace while cutting the heat losses of an open fire by 60 to 90 per cent; the wood stove puts out about five times as much usable heat as the open fire. In the country it is possible to run the stoves on wood obtained by coppicing of the hedgerows, fallen trees, and possibly unwanted ash trees owned by the Forestry Commission, which have already been allowed to fall to make way for new planting.

The value to the renovator of these remarkable stoves lies in the following: the doors on most models may be left open to provide the sight of a real fire; smoke need not be a problem if dry, well-seasoned wood is burned (one advantage of using old timber from building sites); many models will burn hot for up to five hours or so on one filling, and stay alight overnight; some models have facilities for heating hot water systems and several radiators; and finally, there is no need to chop down all the trees in the street to keep warm. Without even having recourse to the supplies of ready-cut firewood (you can never be sure if forests are being decimated with no replanting schemes) available in most areas, the above-mentioned sources can supply all the user's needs. Hence these stoves can be quite a selling point if their location is carefully thought out beforehand. Look out for these models and you will see how they can be both decorative and functional:

—The Kosi Gee and Ophelia by Lange (Danish)
—Some of the Jotuls (Norwegian)

—The Marlborough by Logfires (English).
More details are given in the appendix.

A rough guide to comparative costs:
—Small cast-iron period fireplaces start at around £85.
—Wooden fireplace surrounds, ie mantel and side pieces, start at about £80.
—Log-effect gas fires can be bought for as little as £120.
—Woodburning stoves of reasonable quality start at about £200.

8. The new electrical installation

Instead of wire fuses, fit miniature circuit breakers to the new consumer unit (what some people call the 'fuse box'). Unlike the wire in a fuse, they do not need replacement after blowing when a fault occurs. They switch the current off in the event of a fault, and can be subsequently reset after the problem has been solved simply by switching them on again just like an ordinary light switch. This takes literally one second compared with 10 minutes or so to replace the wire in a fuse, not to mention the time spent hunting for the right fuse wire and going to buy some if you have none left. MCBs are an immense help both to the builder and the future owner of the dwelling.

Summary

This chapter does not pretend to be exhaustive in its discussion of practicalities. You will have plenty of ideas of your own about what to do and what not to do, but the points mentioned here may help to set you thinking about the things which must be considered, both large and small.

Chapter 11 discusses the most important of these issues in relation to completing your first project.

Chapter 10
The Finished Product

Your first project will probably be a conversion into flats. When the work is finished you should have a saleable commodity on your hands.

What makes the property saleable? Try to see it through the eyes of a prospective buyer. Young couples buying the first home of their own will be impressed by a flat which looks fresh, cheerful, spacious and comfortable. A plethora of expensive kitchen gadgets and fittings, immaculately restored period fireplaces, exotic ceiling roses and the like do look impressive, but they all cost a lot to install and are best not indulged in too much on the early projects. A very pleasing effect can be created simply by tastefully finishing off aspects of the work which are essential anyway—there is nothing to beat well-finished basic plasterwork and joinery for giving an elegant appearance to even the most modest of dwellings.

The first impression

Don't forget that, although most of your work will have gone into putting the building itself to rights, the appearance of the property in its surroundings as approached from the street will create an important first impression. Tidy up the garden. If your pocket will run to it, 'landscape' it with a few shrubs and, if possible, a couple of jardinières on the window sills. Repair any damage to garden walls and fences, and give the garden gate a lick of paint. Make good the path leading up to the front entrance, and the front steps. All these things help to enhance the setting of your property. They have a strong impact on the buyer, for they create a more comfortable environment for the home.

The front door gives you an excellent opportunity to show your taste before your clients have even entered the house. Brass door furniture—the doorknob, knocker and letterbox—will give it an elegant appearance and set the tone for what the viewer will see inside.

Builder's finish

In our opinion at this stage of the game it is safest to decorate the entire interior of the property in white, for several reasons:

1. It shows off good new plaster-work to its best advantage, reflecting more light than any other colour, and making the whole place look fresh and cheerful.

2. White makes rooms look spacious, bigger than they really are—a highly desirable quality.

3. White is generally acknowledged to be the standard 'builders' finish', and is less controversial than others. It is notoriously difficult to appeal to other people's tastes with colour schemes of one's own choosing, and it will be a needless waste of time and resources to have to redecorate from scratch if your own brilliant combination of colours should put off would-be buyers. White is neutral and tends to be a 'non-colour', so play safe and use it.

Decorate walls in a recently replastered building with white emulsion; this acknowledges, and will be seen to acknowledge by those who know, ie surveyors acting on behalf of potential buyers, the fact that new plaster takes several months to dry out—there is a saying in the trade that for every inch of thickness of a brick wall you should add another month for drying out, (ie nine months for a 9 inch thick wall, and so on). Emulsion will allow this moisture to dry through the paint to some extent, whereas paper will eventually peel and leave you with a distinctly unimpressive finish to explain away to your clients. Thus, using white emulsion implies that you are aware of this and merely providing what may only turn out to be a temporary but presentable decor.

Original features

We ourselves like to preserve *some* original features of the building, even when finances are hard pressed. The notes in the previous chapter dealt with most aspects of this subject, but it is worth mentioning that if you can salvage nothing else already in the house when you first acquired it, two items may be worth keeping and drawing some attention to in the finished product:

1. Panelled doors
Wooden panelled doors look much more attractive than the oft-fitted flush (flat) ones made from hardboard and cardboard. They feel better, they have the right weight, and although in some cases you may have to put fireproofing in the panels (not difficult) you will find that you will be able to reuse many of the doors already in the house. The odd missing one can be replaced with a second-hand door from your local neighbourhood pine-stripping shop where there will always be spare ones available at a nominal price. Round them off with brass knobs, which will beautifully complement the white paintwork.

2. The original floorboards
Bearing in mind the points made in the previous chapter about floors and having made up complete wooden floors in some rooms, you will find that there are quite large gaps between the old boards due to loss of natural moisture and shrinkage over the years. These gaps can be filled with a mastic filler, easily and quickly applied with a hand gun. The filler remains flexible after it has cured, or 'gone off', allowing for further shrinkage of the boards. It comes in different colours, so you can use a brown mastic if you want it not to show, or white if you want to emphasise the joints.

*NB. A general note on woodwork and
central heating*
Remember that central heating gives a very dry heat
which will cause such loss of moisture content in
wooden fittings of every kind that they will soon warp
and, in the case of panelled assemblies literally tear
themselves apart (this includes the doors and floors,
of course). So do your buyer the courtesy of pointing
out that humidifiers are needed to counteract this
effect, even if you don't actually provide them yourself.

Importance of the kitchen and bathroom

Apart from the general appearance of the interior the
most important rooms to 'get right' in a conversion or
renovation are the kitchen and bathroom. We have
mentioned that lavish appointments are out on the
first projects, but a little style with the essentials will
achieve a good result. Both rooms must be provided
with storage facilities—kitchen worktops and cupboard units, airing cupboards etc, and it is now
possible to buy stylishly finished units in kit form
from very cheap sources; for example, the MFI range
has been much improved of late and yet the prices are
still pegged very low, with realistic wood-grained
finishes and good colour options available on elegant
designs.

In addition to the atmosphere that these units can
help to create, your choice of bathroom suite, kitchen
sink design, wall and floor finishes (probably tiles)
can sell the place almost on their own in many cases.
Style combined with restraint and economy is the
keynote.

Cork floor tiles. Cork tiles pre-sealed with a veneer of
clear pvc are an excellent way to finish the floors of
rooms which are likely to have a lot of water splashed
about in them, and may easily be laid over rough
wooden floors by glueing them to a backing of hardboard which has been nailed to the floor first. While
these tiles are not cheap, the speed at which they can
be laid compensates for this, and their universal

appeal ensures that you won't be putting anyone off by using them. Be sure to buy the tiles which are already coated in pvc—the others are useless. They have no strength and even after varnishing in situ soon become soggy and break up.

Bathroom suites and how to save money on them. A white bathroom suite is considerably cheaper than this year's 'in' colours. Most dealers also do a range of 'budget' colours which cost a little more than white but a lot less than the Kashmir Beiges, Indian Ivories and the like. These budget colours—usually yellows, greens and pinks—can look quite presentable in the right setting, although obviously not as plushy as the luxury colours. Even the clinical look of a white suite can be softened in carefully chosen surroundings.

Carpets. Many estate agents will insist that the only way to sell a property easily is to fit carpets through-out. This is fine, but they are expensive, and the estate agents don't have to foot the bill. Estate agents are keen to make their commission by quick sales, and not necessarily so keen to maximise your profits.

In some cases, fitted carpets may put off would-be buyers who are keen to strip the floors themselves to give the property more of a 'natural' feel. On the other hand, if you decide to patch up the existing boards and leave them ready to be stripped if the buyer wishes, *or* to be carpeted, hence wasting no expenditure on unnecessary preparation, this is often seen by viewers of the property as skimping on the work and again they may be put off if your choice of colours is not to their own taste. Also, old floorboards which may be quite good enough for stripping and varnishing don't look particularly impressive before this has been done, so if you leave them in this condition you also run a risk of putting some people off, even though you may simply be keeping their options open.

It is surprising how little imagination the average homebuyers have in this and other areas of decor—they instantly know what they don't like when they see it, but are less sure about how they would have done it themselves. If you are unfortunate enough to have the more demanding kind of viewer looking at your property, it is worth remembering that invariably the most awkward ones are those who are least likely ever to get around to buying at all. It is really not worth spending hours with this kind of client and offering to make all kinds of alterations to get a sale. They are notoriously unreliable, and the next time they see you they will probably have changed their mind anyway. Fortunately, one learns how to spot them a mile off at an early stage of the game and behave accordingly.

The decision as to what to do with the floor treatment in the property is one of the trickiest of the project. It's really for you to weigh up the cheaper alternatives against what really suits the 'feel' of the property best; we *have* sold flats with floors hardboarded ready to receive carpets, but it's a hit-and-miss business. The safest colours for fitted carpets are beiges.

Lighting. It's tempting to let your imagination run riot on the lighting, with carriage lamps outside the front door, brass wall lamps in the living room, and panoramic strip lighting under the worktops in the kitchen. But your tastes may be different from those of your buyer, and it is not a pleasant business, in a complete conversion or renovation with neatly finished floors, to have to pull them up and re-run cables. This is what you will be faced with if your fabulously expensive wall lighting arrangements leave him or her cold and a centre ceiling light is preferred.

Unfortunately, any attempt at pre-wiring to cater for any of several different lighting positions still doesn't solve the problem—in our experience things still seem to be 'in the wrong place'. It is better to eat humble pie and stick with straightforward centre lamp positions as far as possible until you progress to catering for the penthouse set!

Consumer law

Consumer law has only a minimal effect on property sales. Once he has the surveyor's report the buyer is deemed to be in possession of all the relevant facts regarding the property, and the purchase is then made 'as seen and approved'.

However, if you have installed guaranteed items such as a damp-proof course, central heating, kitchen appliances etc, it may be necessary, as a condition of sale, to agree to repair or replace defective parts during the guarantee period, especially if you have installed these items yourself. So make sure you keep all receipts relating to guaranteed items in a separate file.

If you employed contractors to install, for example, central heating, the buyer of your property may have to arrange through you the implementation of any work under guarantee, as you were the one who initially paid for the installation.

Guarantees for damp-proofing and dry rot protection ought to be transferable to the owner of the property. The reason for this is that such guarantees are usually lengthy (20 years or more) and the property could be sold and resold several times during the guarantee period. So you should make sure when employing damp-proofing contractors that their guarantees *are* transferable.

You should offer guarantees to your buyer on anything which you bought or installed that carries a manufacturer's guarantee. This may involve you in a little time but should cost you nothing more than the occasional phone call or letter.

Chapter 11
Marketing and Selling

Fixing the selling price

If you researched your project thoroughly at the start you will have known all along what sort of price to expect for the finished product.

However, what you planned on paper doesn't always compare with what happens in practice. You may find that the quality of your renovation surpasses the standards you set yourself initially, which will, of course, increase the value of your property. On the other hand, the finished product may be less than you hoped for. The uncertainty of the exact final value put upon the conversion is one very good reason for not over-estimating the selling price when you do your initial costing.

It is the actual finished product that your buyer looks at, and with a critical eye.

The best way to get a market value put on your property is to get one or more local estate agents to look at it, whether you intend to use them to sell the property or not.

Being used to selling properties in your area, they can give you an immediate idea of market value, nearly always based on what, for example, a 'two-bedroom flat in the area' is worth, with added points for garden, carpets, fitments, quality of finish etc.

Having decided on this market value, it is then necessary to fix an advertising price. This should always be over and above the market value because anybody interested in buying is more than likely to make an offer which is nearly always below the asking price. This little charade ensures that you get somewhere near to the market value for your property, and the buyer is happy because he has achieved a 'discount'.

If you are lucky enough to have several people making offers at the same time you are in a strong position, and can hold out for the highest bid.

It is highly likely that the person who wishes to buy your property will have to obtain a mortgage. This will take time to arrange, so if you have somebody interested in buying who has cash available (maybe from a recent house sale), it is well worth giving them special consideration, even if their offer is slightly lower. The faster you sell the better it is for you.

Methods of selling

As mentioned earlier, in the case of conversion into flats it is sometimes possible to finish one flat in advance of the others and sell it, even though the rest of the flats are far from finished. A prospective buyer may exchange contracts subject to completion, which will normally entitle you to a 10 per cent deposit. An inflow of cash at this stage of the renovation is not to be sneezed at, and if buyers are that anxious for your flats it proves that you have chosen your area and layout well.

Once your property is finished you will want to sell it as quickly as possible. A property sitting on the market for any length of time will cost you money in the form of bank interest and deterioration. So before the work is completely finished you must decide how to sell—or market—your property.

There are various choices open to you, and these are:

1. Selling to friends
This is a satisfactory way to sell as you avoid advertising and estate agents' fees.

2. Advertising yourself
National newspapers, local papers and property magazines are relatively cheap forms of advertising and it is well worth trying this form of advertising before any other. The big Sunday papers bring in the best response.

3. Computer selling

For a fixed fee (approximately £2 or £3 per £1000 selling price) they will circulate details of your property to people interested in that type of dwelling, for as long as necessary.

4. Property shops

You put a card in their window with property details. Good value for money, but reaches fewer people.

5. 'For sale' board

As well as advertising elsewhere, you can erect your own 'for sale' board outside the property. You can put on it as much detail as you like about accommodation, and you can also include the price—something that estate agents' boards don't often do.

6. Auctions

These are not the best places to sell renovated property. Auctions are better for selling cheap un-mortgageable properties.

7. Estate agents

Last but not least. Definitely the best way to tap the largest possible market in the shortest possible time is to put your property with several estate agents (not just one). They are obviously very experienced in selling property quickly.

The drawback with using estate agents is, of course, the large fee that they require to sell your property. You can pay as much as 3 per cent of the selling price. This means that on the sale of three flats at £40,000 each you would pay £3600 in agents' fees, and that is a large slice out of your profits, so if you can sell by other means—do so.

Freeholds/Leaseholds

When putting your property up for sale, you will have to decide whether or not to sell the freehold.

If you wish to keep the freehold yourself it means selling your property on a lease; the length of the lease then has to be decided. It ought not to be less than 99 years. By keeping the freehold yourself the value of the property will be reduced, and you will be responsible for collecting ground rent and possibly liable for some of the general upkeep of the property. It is generally better, therefore, to include the freehold in the sale of the property.

In the case of a single property, renovation of a house for example, this is easily done.

In a flats conversion it is not quite so straightforward. Leases are normally granted on each flat and then someone has to own the freehold. This someone could be yourself, or one of the leaseholders, or all leaseholders could jointly own the freehold. Your solicitor will advise when drawing up the leases, and in consultation with the buyers and yourself.

In our opinion it is better for you that the freehold is sold with the property.

Chapter 12

Legal Requirements Relating to the Business

Company law

If you propose to conduct your business as a limited company, you will be required to register it with Companies House. You can decide on a name, and purchase the company for about £100. You can if you wish buy an existing company, but this is generally more expensive and complicated.

One of the most useful features of a limited company is that it gives you the protection of limited liability: if your business should go seriously awry, you will not then be held personally responsible for paying any outstanding debts still owing after all the company funds have been exhausted. This contrasts with, for example, running your business as a sole trader, or in a partnership, where your own personal finances could be seized by a debtor.

The price you have to pay for this protection is more red tape. You are legally required to issue a certain number of share certificates to yourself and partners (these will not actually be partners in the legal sense—they will probably be your fellow directors in the company. In legal terms a partner is part of 'a partnership', which, as mentioned above, is less well protected than a limited company). You must also appoint directors, hold annual general meetings and send 'company returns' to Companies House every year. You will also need to appoint a company secretary—here you may be able to kill two birds with one stone by appointing your solicitor to this post if he is amenable. This will cut down the amount of liaison necessary between people, saving time and money.

The company will need a Memorandum and

Articles of Association, which is merely a description of the trade(s) which the company is legally entitled to carry on. Your solicitor will prove his worth once again by dealing with this for you.

Apart from such general obligations pertaining to the limited company, the property renovator is compelled by the law to conform to other conditions and restraints.

The local authority

You will have to carry out any work done on your property in accordance with local authority requirements, including building regulations and the by-laws.

1. Compulsory repairs

These may be required if the Health Department has put an order on the premises condemning it as unfit for habitation. If the owner fails to carry out these repairs within the authority's specified deadline, it is free to have the work done and charge him for it — at a much higher figure than it would have cost him to organise it himself.

If it is considered dangerous as well, the authority may even have slapped a demolition order on the property.

If an order for repairs *has* been put on the house, don't automatically be put off buying it. Most of these you will be aware of and will be intending to carry out anyway. However, it pays to have a thorough investigation done in this area (which is taken in by your solicitor's local authority search — see Chapter 4), as the vendor and his solicitor may well not be falling over themselves to point out these shortcomings to you.

In some cases, however, these orders are somewhat over-zealously applied; a couple of years ago we were interested in purchasing a mews cottage which seemed to have a lot going for it until we discovered that, in addition to our planned works, we would be forced to carry out re-roofing and major under-pinning, neither of which we considered necessary. A health order was in force. The project was, therefore, not financially viable, so we had to look elsewhere for our next purchase. A grant might have been available for these items but in view of the problems we describe in Chapter 2 with reference to grants, we gave it a miss.

2. Searches and conveyancing

At the beginning of the project, the local authority search is required by law. As things stand at present the search and conveyancing are carried out by the solicitor in most cases. You can do them yourself but they take some getting to grips with.

3. Contracts and solicitors

At present each party in a property transaction must have his own contract drawn up, which he then passes to the other party for signature. Also, each party must have his own solicitor. There may be new legislation on the way enabling just one document and one solicitor to perform the transaction, thereby saving both vendor and buyer money, time and frustration. The legal profession will still manage to scrape a living, even so, and it will leave a little more money in the renovator's pocket for the work in hand.

4. Listed buildings

Another control you may have to contend with is the listing of buildings which are considered to be of architectural and/or historic interest. The grade 1 or 2 listing of a building means that anyone repairing or modifying it may be obliged to spend money on restoring some of its historic architectural features to the specification given by the relevant DOE department. This work may well have to be financed out of the renovator's own pocket, as listed building repairs grants are becoming increasingly hard to obtain (see Chapter 2 on raising finance).

The sort of features involved in this kind of architecture are certain kinds of mouldings and decoration, eg pilasters, porticoes, colonnades and corbels; typical glazing patterns characteristic of definite periods of architecture, eg Regency, Georgian, Victorian, Edwardian (often, over the years, repairs will have been carried out which mix incompatible styles, and the historic buildings officials will press to have the original period features restored); and details like front door styles and garden railings.

Most of these regulations are applied much more rigidly to the outside of the building rather than the inside, certainly on the properties which come within the newly established renovator's funds. When your fortunes have grown enough for you to start renovating Scottish castles, it will be a different matter!

5. Highways regulations
A more mundane legal restraint on you, but none the less one to be reckoned with once you start the renovation proper, is exerted by the highways regulations.

During the course of the work you will be receiving deliveries of heavy, bulky materials—bricks, sand, cement, slates, lintels etc—which cannot be moved or stored easily. A vast quantity of rubble and rubbish will have to be removed from the site by skips or trucks. You must observe the by-laws by obtaining a permit for any materials or skips to be left in the road. The only strings attached are that they carry a time limit. Once a permit has lapsed it must be renewed if still needed.

The highways officers are surprisingly quick to notice even a few odd bricks left on the pavement for a couple of days, so get yourself covered before they show up. Delays due to this kind of interruption can be irritating and disruptive to the progress of the job.

In some circumstances a permit is also needed for scaffolding erected over a pavement.

Insurance

1. Public liability insurance
Any building site is, by the nature of the work, prone to accidents from time to time. You must have an insurance against any injury sustained by a member of the public in an incident on or near your site. Any-

thing might happen—a passer-by might be hit by a falling scaffold board—and a large claim would severely detract from the project, let alone make a dent in funds if the worst came to the worst.

The law requires any subcontractor who wishes to obtain a Tax Exemption Certificate (see Chapter 7) to take out such an insurance. The minimum cover is about £250,000. As main contractor, you should take out your own, even though your 'subbies' may have them. The premium may be as little as £50 a year.

2. Insuring yourself and your tools
While you are at it, insure yourself for loss of earnings due to injury, and your tools against theft; at least *one* of these items is irreplaceable.

3. Insuring the property
If you have a bank loan the bank will require you to take out an insurance against damage to the property during your ownership. They will be happy to organise one for you. In any event, you *should* organise cover for the premises or you might find the carpet well and truly pulled from under you financially if anything should befall it.

Chapter 13

How to Use Profits and Plan Ahead

Of those that set themselves up in the property business by borrowing capital, all but the most adventurous will start by buying one property, doing what they want to it, and selling it before they contemplate anything further. This is certainly the safest and surest way and is to be recommended.

Having completed and sold your first property, however, and assuming that it has worked reasonably well, you will be keen to go on to the next one.

It is still advisable, and probably necessary financially, to stick to one property at a time. You would need to build up considerable capital and expertise to be able to handle several properties at once. The amount of expertise depends upon the individual, of course, and you could be faced with the option of expanding your business and borrowing more money, or staying with the smaller conversions and using your profits.

Assessing your first renovation

If you made a reasonable profit on your first renovation and you wish to go on to something bigger and better, bear in mind that you should still keep well within your financial limits. You will in any case have to consult with your bank and/or backers.

Your financial backers will naturally evaluate your success in terms of profit, quality of renovation, ease of selling etc, and assuming that you have managed your first project competently, will be bound to want to continue with their support. A successful businessman will always attract backers.

With your first property out of the way, the risk is that you become over-confident.

Sit down with your site diary, works programme, financial projections, estimates and costings, and evaluate for yourself how successful you were. Note down where mistakes were made; where estimates were wildly out; where, perhaps, something was not allowed for at all. The experience gained from this will help enormously with your next project.

This is also the time to reflect on the contractors that you used. How punctual were they? How competent? How many call-backs were necessary to put something right? Would you use them again?

You can also assess your own ability at doing certain jobs, and whether it would have been quicker and cheaper to employ specialists. It may have been that you wished to do the work yourself in order to gain practical knowledge. If you have achieved this it will benefit you next time whether you do the work yourself, or not.

By renovating one property at a time and assessing your results in this way after each one, you will become very experienced and discover that expanding your business will present little difficulty.

You may be tempted to try and work out a comprehensive plan for the next five to ten years. Forget it. You must treat each project as a separate entity, and allow events to take their course. 'The best laid plans . . .'

Using profits

When your first project is finished and sold you will have a large amount of money in the bank. Some of it will be borrowed money, some profit. What you do with that money will depend to some extent on how you set up the finances in the first place. For example, if you have not been paying yourself a regular wage (just expenses), you may need to draw some money for yourself. Your backers or partners may need to do the same.

You are faced with the problem of how much, if any, money to withdraw, and how much to reinvest, or roll over, into your next property. Obviously, the more money you put into the next property the less you will have to borrow, and the greater the possibility of tackling something larger. The bank may agree to increase the amount they will lend. In a purely business sense, it is better to reinvest as much as possible in your next property, and it will look good on paper.

If you do intend to draw out some of the profit (as opposed to expenses) it is a good idea to have a chat with your accountant about the best way to do it, as you will attract taxation in various forms, and he will explain how to keep it to a minimum.

There is another way of using profits, although you may have to wait a year or two and acquire some capital to make it possible. Assuming that you already own the house you live in you can, in addition, buy a house or cottage (maybe in the country), modernise it to a reasonable standard, and then hang on to it until you retire (it might be sooner than you think).

The benefit of doing this is that when you do retire, you can sell either the house you have been living in, or the one you have been keeping as an investment. This provides you with a sizeable capital sum to supplement your fixed pension. The longer you have owned your investment property the more it will be worth.

You will be liable for capital gains tax on one of the properties but it is still worth doing.

Also, of course, by living in town and buying your investment property in the country, you have the choice of either place to live when you retire, and a weekend retreat in the meantime.

New technology

New products and materials are continually coming on to the market in the building industry, and you will obviously be tempted to use some of them. You will need to be careful about how far you go with new materials, as a lot of potential buyers of your properties will hold traditional views and will not be impressed if new products have not been tried and tested.

Plastics, for example, are increasingly being used in place of traditional materials for windows, roofing products, tile and brick-effect walls, central heating pipes, and so on.

Glass fibre, although not new, is increasingly being used instead of plaster and sand/cement when replacing or newly installing porticoes, cornices, columns, pilasters etc. It has the advantage of light weight, and speed and ease of installation. It also requires no maintenance.

The microchip is also making inroads into the home (particularly in electrical control equipment and security systems), and in the next five to ten years is bound to affect the design and renovation of buildings.

Some technological breakthroughs appear on the scene and then remain static due to difficulties in application. A good example is solar heating. The theory is fine. Installation in a suitable property is not difficult. The prospect of generating your own hot water is exciting. Yet there are just not enough suitable properties. When you need the hot water most (in the winter to run your heating system), there is insufficient sunshine to supply your heating needs independently. You still need the back-up of a gas or oil-fired system. There can be some benefit from hot water in the summer months, but at this operational level it can take years to recover the installation cost.

New technology and products always take time to become accepted into everyday use, and before using anything untried in your properties you will have to decide for yourself what is acceptable and what is not.

Keeping in touch

While attempting to buy your first property you will have encountered a few estate agents. Some will have been friendly and efficient, others maybe a bit offhand and unconcerned. It is in your interests to keep in regular contact with estate agents, preferably the friendly ones. Stopping off at their offices occasionally will keep you in touch with the market generally, and them in touch with progress on your property.

Agents may be able to suggest minor additions or

improvements to your renovation, as they are continually meeting buyers, and know what is popular and fashionable. They will also know whether the type of property you are renovating is increasing in demand and value, even while you are working on it. If it is, it may enable you to upgrade the property further, with the prospect of increased profit.

During these chats the subject of further suitable properties for conversion will undoubtedly arise. Such properties frequently come on to the estate agents' books, and if you are in regular contact you will be among the first to hear about them. Even though you may not be in a position to buy your next property there and then, there is no harm in going to have a look at those that sound promising. 'Just looking' will help you keep your ear to the ground and your mind focused on what your future moves ought to be.

Appendixes

Appendix 1
Useful Addresses

National telephone dialling codes are given, though local codes may differ.

Local councils and Chambers of Commerce can be good sources of help and information.

General

Alliance of Small Firms and Self-Employed People
42 Vine Road, East Molesey, Surrey KT8 9LF;
01-979 2293
Bathroom and Shower Centre
204 Great Portland Street, London W1; 01-388 7631
British Gas
Rivermill House, 152 Grosvenor Road, London SW1;
01-821 1444
British Safety Council
62 Chancellors Road, London W6; 01-741 1231
British Standards Institution
2 Park Street, London W1; 01-629 9000
Building Centres
26 Store Street, London WC1; 01-637 8361
115 Portland Street, Manchester; 061-236 9802
Earl Street, Coventry; 0203 25555
18 Cumberland Place, Southampton; 0303 27350
Hope Street, Liverpool; 051-700 8566
and other major towns and cities
Central Electricity Generating Board
Sudbury House, 15 Newgate Street, London
WC1A 7AU; 01-248 1202
Consumers Association
14 Buckingham Street, London WC2;
01-839 1222
Electrical Contractors Association
34 Palace Court, London W2 4HY; 01-229 1266

Health and Safety Commission
Regina House, 259 Old Marylebone Road, London
NW1 5RR; 01-723 1262
Health and Safety Executive
25 Chapel Street, London NW1 5DT; 01-262 3277
HM Customs and Excise
VAT Administration Directorate, King's Beam
House, Mark Lane, London EC3R 7HE; 01-626 1515
Inland Revenue
Contact your local Inspector of Taxes to register for
PAYE and find out where your Local Employers'
Unit is for all necessary paperwork (PAYE and
National Insurance).
Registrar of Companies
Companies House, Crown Way, Maindy, Cardiff
CF4 3UZ; 0222 388588
102 George Street, Edinburgh EH2 3DJ;
031-225 5774
43-7 Chichester Street, Belfast BT1 4RJ;
0232 234121
Solid Fuel Advisory Service
Hobart House, Grosvenor Place, London SW1;
01-235 2020

Firms providing damp proofing and timber treatment service

Dampcoursing Ltd
10 Dorset Road, London N15; 01-802 2233
Peter Cox Ltd
Wandle Way, Mitcham, Surrey; 01-640 1151
Rentokil Ltd
16 Dover Street, London W1; 01-493 0061

Manufacturers of products in general use

Airflow Developments—airvents for rooms and
toilets
Lancaster Road, High Wycombe, Bucks HP12 3QP;
0494 25252
Alpine Co Ltd—double glazing
Alpine House, Honeypot Lane, London NW9;
01-204 3393

Armitage Shanks Ltd—bathroom equipment
303 High Holborn, London WC1; 01-405 9663
Barlo Products Ltd—radiators
Barlo House, Foundry Lane, Horsham, West Sussex;
0403 62342
Black & Decker Ltd—power tools
Cannon Road, Maidenhead, Berks; 062 882 2130
Celcon Ltd—thermal building blocks
Celcon House, 289 High Holborn, London
WC1V 7HU; 01-242 9766
Crabtree Electrical Industries Ltd—electrical
equipment
Tuition House, St George's Road, London SW19;
01-947 8281
Cuprinol Ltd—treatments and stains for wood
Adderwell, Frome, Somerset BA11 1NL; 0373 65151
Delmar nmc Ltd—decorative mouldings
Manor Royal, Crawley, Sussex RH10 2XQ;
0293 546251
Everest—double glazing
Everest House, Sopers Road, Cuffley, Herts;
070 72 63535
Faral Tropical 80—high output radiators
Door-to-Door Depot, Gatwick Road, Crawley,
Sussex; 0293 541705
FEB Ltd—sealants, adhesives, mortar additives
Albany House, Swinton Hall Road, Swinton,
Manchester M27 1DT; 061-794 7411
Franke (UK) Ltd—sinks
International Office Centre, Styal Road,
Manchester; 061-436 6280
Glow-worm TI Ltd—central heating boilers
Nottingham Road, Belper, Derby DE5 1JT;
077382 4141
Gyproc Ltd—plasterboard and insulation
Whitehouse Industrial Estate, Runcorn, Cheshire
WA7 3DP; 0928 712627
Hodkin & Jones (Sheffield) Ltd—decorative
mouldings
515 Queens Road, Sheffield S2 4DS; 0742 56121
ICI Dulux Ltd—paint and woodcare products
Wexham Road, Slough, Berks; 0753 31151

Ideal Standard Ltd—bathroom equipment
PO Box 60, Kingston upon Hull HU5 4JE;
0482 46461
Kango Wolf—power tools
Hanger Lane, London W5; 01-937 3444
Key Terrain Ltd—plastic soil, waste and rainwater systems
Aylesford, Maidstone, Kent ME20 7PJ; 0622 77811
MFI Furniture Centres—budget kitchens and furniture
Highams Park Industrial Estate, Larkshall Road,
London E4; 01-531 8874
Mira (Walker Crossweller & Co Ltd)—showers
Whaddon Works, Cheltenham, Glos GL52 5EP;
0242 27953
MK Electric Ltd—electrical equipment
Shrubbery Road, London N9; 01-807 5151
Myson Domestic Products Ltd—radiators and heating equipment
Ongar, Essex CM5 9RE; 0277 362222
PC Henderson Ltd—garage doors and sliding doors
Tangeant Road, Romford, Essex RM3 8UL;
04023 45555
Permanite Ltd—roofing bitumens and solutions
Mead Lane, Hertford, Herts; 0992 50511
Pilkington Glass Ltd—glass manufacturers
Selwyn House, Cleveland Row, London SW1;
01-930 5672
Potterton International Ltd—central heating equipment
Portobello Works, Emscote Road, Warwick
CV34 5QU; 0926 43420
Rawlplug—wall and cavity fixings
PO Box 64, Borehamwood, Herts WD6 1BA
Rothervale Joinery Ltd—windows and joinery;
RSM Works, Hallcroft Road, Retford, Notts;
0742 693291
Runtalrad (1970) Ltd—stylish, made-to-order radiators
Ridgeway Industrial Estate, Ridgeway Road, Iver,
Bucks; 0753 654142

Sadolin (UK) Ltd—wood protection
Tower Close, St Peter's Industrial Park,
Huntingdon, Cambs PE18 7DR; 0480 50041
Solarbo Fitments Ltd—kiln-dried pine doors and
kitchen units
Unit 4, 61 Ebury Street, London SW1; 01-730 2192
Sphinx Tiles—range of wall and floor tiles
Bath Road, Thatcham, Newbury, Berks; 0635 65475
Stelrad Group Ltd—central heating equipment
PO Box 103, National Avenue, Kingston upon Hull
HU5 4JN; 0482 492251
Thermalite Ltd—thermal building blocks
Station Road, Coleshill, Birmingham B46 1HP;
0675 62081
Thorn EMI Ltd—central heating equipment
Eastern Avenue, Team Valley Trading Estate,
Gateshead, Tyne and Wear NE11 0PG; 0632 872211
Twyfords Bathrooms—bathroom equipment
PO Box 23, Stoke on Trent, Staffs ST4 7AL;
0782 29531
Unibond Ltd—mortar additives, sealants and
adhesives
Tuscam Way Industrial Estate, Camberley, Surrey;
0276 685345
Verine Products Co Ltd—decorative mouldings
Folly Faunts House, Goldhanger, Maldon, Essex
CM9 8AP; 0621 88611
Vogue Bathrooms—bathroom equipment
Bilston, West Midlands WV14 8UA; 0902 432121
Volex Electrical Products Ltd—electrical
equipment and accessories
Accessories Division, Leigh Road, Hindley Green,
Lancashire WN2 4XY; 0942 57100

Large builders' merchants

C P Hart & Sons, Builders' and Plumbers'
Merchants
Arch 213 Newham Terrace, Hercules Road, London
SE1; 01-928 3812
Magnet & Southerns, Windows, Joinery, Doors and
Accessories

Head office: Magnet Joinery, Keighley, W. Yorks;
0535 661133

Head office: Southerns Evans Ltd—Widnes,
Cheshire; 051-424 5500; over 240 branches
nationwide

Sandell Perkins plc, Builders', Plumbers' and Timber
Merchants

Cobtree House, Forstal Road, Maidstone, Kent
ME20 7AG; 0622 70111; branches throughout
London and the south of England

J H Sankey & Son Ltd, Builders', Plumbers' and
Heating Merchants

London office: 389 Edgware Road, London NW2;
01-450 2536; many branches

UBM Goslett, Builders' Merchants

Warwick Place, High Street, Uxbridge, Middx;
0895 38200; and branches

M Wisepart Ltd, Builders', Heating, Plumbers'
Merchants and Kitchens

Factory Lane, London N17; 01-801 2161; and
branches

Tool and equipment hire shops

HSS hire service shops
over 70 branches and depots in England, Wales and
Scotland

PB Power tools
Head office: Long Wood Road, Trafford Park,
Manchester M17 1PZ; 061-872 6817; branches in
Bolton, Liverpool, London, Manchester and
Tarporley

Do-it-yourself shops

B&Q
DIY Supercentre, 3 King Street, London W3;
01-992 1182

Texas Homecare DIY Stores
Head office: Cline Road, London N11; 01-368 0141;
and branches

WHS Do-it-all; branches of WH Smith & Son Ltd
Wickes DIY Superstores
53 Plough Lane, London SW17; 01-947 9817; and
branches

Some manufacturers and distributors of woodburning stoves

Jotul (Norwegian)
Sole importers UK and Ireland: Jotul Stoves
(Norcem UK Ltd), Old Bath Road, Charville, Reading
RG10 9QS; 0734 340223
Lange (Danish)
'Earthworks', Ludlow, Hereford; 0584 2010
Logfires Ltd (English)
Southern Stoves, South Street, Dorking, Surrey;
0306 883201

Appendix 2
Further Reading

Buying and selling houses

Bradshaw's Guide to DIY House Buying, Selling and Conveyancing (Castle Books)
Do It Yourself Conveyancing, Robert T Steele (David and Charles)
The Legal Side of Buying a House (Consumers' Association)

Grants

Home Improvement Grants: a guide for home owners, landlords and tenants, Department of the Environment, housing booklet No 14 (HMSO)
Housing Grants, Nigel Hawkins (Kogan Page)

The building regulations

The Building Regulations (HMSO)
The Building Regulations Explained and Illustrated, W S Whyte and Vincent Powell-Smith (Crosby Lockwood Staples)
Guide to the Building Regulations, A J Elder (Architectural Press)

General practical information

Alteration or Conversion of Houses, J F Garner (Oyez)
Brickwork 1, W G Walsh (Hutchinson)
The Complete Home Carpenter, (Marshall Cavendish)
A Concise Building Encylopaedia, T Corkhill (Pitman)

How to Restore and Improve Your Victorian House,
Alan Johnson (David and Charles)
The Penguin Dictionary of Building, John S Scott
(Penguin)
The Reader's Digest Do-it-yourself Manual,
(Reader's Digest)
Repairing Houses, Trevor James (Sphere)
The Sunday Times Book of DIY (Sphere)

Electrics

Home Electrics, Julian Worthington (Orbis)
Rewiring a House, Geoffrey Arnold (Burdett
Publications)
Ring Circuits, Geoffrey Arnold (Burdett
Publications)

Heating

Do Your Own Central Heating Installation, Trevor
Crabtree (Foulsham)

Layout and decor

The House Book, Terence Conran (Mitchell Beazley)
The Kitchen Book, Terence Conran (Mitchell
Beazley)

Lighting

Home Decorating Using Light, Harry Butler
(Marshall Cavendish)

Other relevant titles from Kogan Page

The Guardian Guide to Running a Small Business,
4th edn, Clive Woodcock
Law for the Small Business, 4th edn, Patricia Clayton
Part-time Work, Judith Humphries
Raising Finance, Clive Woodcock
Understand Your Accounts, A St J Price
Working for Yourself, 6th edn, Godfrey Golzen

Glossary of technical terms used in the text

Architrave. The ornamental moulding round a door or window opening, usually covering the joint between the plaster and framing.

Bolster. A bricklayer's cutting chisel, with a blade 2 to 5 inches wide.

Colonnade. A series of columns forming the side of a narrow covered path outside a building. The columns are bridged by lintels.

Corbel. A projecting support on the face of a wall, often, but not always, decorative as well as functional.

Cornice. A horizontal projecting moulding at the top of framing, or at the junction of wall and ceiling, or on the facade of a building.

Cove. A hollow moulding in the form of a quarter circle or ellipse, often used at the junction of wall and ceiling.

Flashing. Sheet lead, zinc or copper fitted to prevent water from penetrating the joints where a vertical surface, eg a wall of chimney stack, projects through a roof.

Joist. Horizontal timbers which carry the floors and ceilings; traditionally made of wood, but see *RSJ*.

Lintel. A horizontal beam across an opening, usually carrying the wall above. Again, traditionally of wood but now usually reinforced concrete (available ready-made).

Pilaster. A thin, rectangular pier projecting from the face of a wall.

Portico. A porch with its roof supported by columns.

RSJ. A joist made of rolled steel, usually used to support the weight bearing down where a wall has been removed (available ready-made).

Screed. A thin, ie 2 or 3 inch layer of concrete flooring, laid over the main 4 to 6 inches deep concrete floor slab. Pipework and electric cables are concealed in it, and it is trowelled to a smooth finish to receive carpets or floor tiles.

Skirting. A moulded decorative finish between the wall and floor, usually in wood but sometimes in concrete or plaster.

Soaker. A piece of lead or zinc formed into a right angle and bonded with slates or similar to make a watertight joint between a wall and roof. Stepped flashings are used over the soakers.

Tongued and grooved. A form of planking. Each plank has a tongue in one edge and a groove in the other. The tongues and grooves on adjacent planks interlock with each other.

Wainscoting. Wall panelling; also used to refer to skirtings.

Index